# Dimple
## Dares to
# Ask

Story by:

# Bola Dada

This is a work of fiction. Names, characters, and businesses are the products of the author's imagination. Except for public figures and pandemic-related events documented in recent history, any resemblance to actual events and persons, living or dead, is purely coincidental.

No part of this publication may be reproduced, distributed or transmitted in any form or by any means, including photocopying, recording, or other electronic or mechanical methods, without the prior written permission of the publisher, except in the case of brief quotations embodied in critical reviews and certain other non-commercial uses permitted by copyright law.

All rights reserved.

The moral right of the author has been asserted.

Scripture quotations are taken from:
The *King James Version* of the Bible.

THE HOLY BIBLE, NEW INTERNATIONAL VERSION®, NIV® Copyright © 1973, 1978, 1984, 2011 by Biblica, Inc.® Used by permission. All rights reserved worldwide.

Scripture quotations marked NLT are taken from the *Holy Bible*, New Living Translation, copyright © 1996, 2004, 2015 by Tyndale House Foundation. Used by permission of Tyndale House Publishers, Inc., Carol Stream, Illinois 60188. All rights reserved.

Book cover design and illustration by Hatice Bayramoglu
https://www.3d2dizayn.com

Editorial Services by Heritage Editing Services
www.heritageediting.com

Published by The Heritage Publishers

Dada, Bola

Email address: Adebola.Dada1@outlook.com

© 2022 by Bola Dada

# CONTENTS

About the book .................................................................. v

Dedication........................................................................ vii

Chapter 1: The End of Term
– 'Where is Dimple'?........................................................1

Chapter 2: Holiday with Mum
- 'What are the best places to visit?'..............................9

Chapter 3: The Time Bridge Squad
- 'What is a virus?' ........................................................17

Chapter 4: A Present for Dimple
– 'Where is The Time Bridge Squad?' .........................21

Chapter 5: Returning Home
- 'How Long is our Flight?' ..........................................27

Chapter 6: Nana plays the piano for her friends
– 'What is Lockdown?' .................................................31

Chapter 7: Clap for the NHS and our carers -
'Where is everyone tonight?'........................................45

Chapter 8: Learning away from School
– 'Why is the internet connection slow?' .....................49

Chapter 9: Mum at work
- 'Where are the family members?' .............................57

Chapter 10: The End of Year 6
- 'Why is there no school trip?' ................... 67

Chapter 11: Food Rationing
- 'Why are the shelves empty?' ................... 75

Chapter 12: Exam Results
- 'What grades will Adam get?' ................... 83

Chapter 13: Happy Birthday, Dimple
– 'Why is Mum shouting my name?' ........... 91

Chapter 14: Little Chef Dimple
- 'What is in the oven?' ............................... 99

Chapter 15: Family Christmas
– 'Where is the Turkey?' ............................ 105

Chapter 16: Nana gets her vaccine
– 'Does your arm hurt, Nana?' ................... 111

Chapter 17: Hands-Face-Space
- 'How will I remember the rules?' ............ 119

Chapter 18: Hands – Face – Space … and
Fresh Air - 'Can I go to the mall please?' ......... 123

Chapter 19: Family Holiday
– 'Are we back to normal?' ........................ 139

Glossary .................................................... 149

Bibliography .............................................. 151

About the Author ....................................... 153

## ABOUT THE BOOK

'*Dimple dares to ask*' is a recollection of events that happened during the Covid-19 crisis, told through the eyes of a 12-year-old girl. The pandemic has affected everyone on earth, with some people experiencing the loss of more than one family member. Others have even lost generations to the virus.

We should not undermine the seriousness of the experience just because the story is told from a child's perspective. Covid-19 remains one of the deadliest viruses to invade the earth. Research is ongoing to find out more about the virus, and it is still a mystery.

I hope to encapsulate the pandemic experience as a resource for young ones who may not understand what is currently going on, and future generations. We should not forget this significant era in our history.

Bereavement, isolation and fear are triggering mental health issues in many, due to the pandemic and consequent lockdowns. The rainbow on the front cover is a symbol of hope. My desire is that this book offers hope despite the darkness they may see or feel right now.

I hope you enjoy reading about Dimple. As you do so, think of the many sacrifices we as individuals have made in this period.

I thank God for the insight to write this book and hope it blesses every soul that reads it.

# DEDICATION

This book is dedicated to all those who have lost loved ones to or are battling Covid themselves. May we all see the light at the end of the tunnel very soon.

Amen.

*Dimple Dares to Ask*

# CHAPTER 1

## THE END OF TERM – 'WHERE IS DIMPLE'?

*December 2019*

'Hurry up, everyone! We're going to be late!' Dimple yells, grabbing the front doorknob. 'Mum, Dad, Nana, Adam! WHERE ARE YOU?'

The younger child of James and Gloria Robinson, Dimple Robinson is a bubbly 11-year-old girl. At 5ft tall, she has a beautiful chocolate complexion and a particularly striking dimple on her left cheek. She twitches and stretches her neck to look up the stairs leading to the upper part of the house.

'We're going to be fine, love,' Dad shouts back from his room. 'It's only a short drive to your school, and there will be no traffic at this time of the day.'

Dimple sighs. 'But, Dad, other parents will be driving to school for our Christmas play too.'

'She's right, James,' Mum says, examining her face at her dressing table mirror in the middle of the bedroom. 'Some workers will also be heading home around this hour.'

Gloria Robinson, Dimple's mum, is a light-skinned lady in her early forties. 5ft 8ins, her black wavy curls reach down to her shoulders. She is wearing a pair of black slacks and a cream ruffle neck blouse. Now a nurse who loves to look after sick people, Gloria won the 'Fresh Talent' contest of her local borough at the age of twenty-one.

She adds a minimal amount of make-up to her smooth oval, crease-free face; pulls on a pair of black, low-heeled shoes and heads out of the bedroom, knocking on Adam's door as she heads down the stairs to an impatient Dimple who is hopping from one foot to another.

'Adam, c'mon. Your sister is going to be late if we don't leave the house now.'

'Dad isn't even ready yet,' Adam says from behind his bedroom door. 'He takes more time to get ready than anyone else in this house. Anyway, I can always meet you at the school.'

'No, we are going together as a family,' Mum tells him. 'Hurry up! You know how much this means to your sister.'

Dimple rushes back into the living room, announcing her orders at the top of her voice. 'Hurry up, everyone! The programme starts at 7pm prompt!' She cuts across the sliding door into Nana's room. 'Let's go, Nana. I'm going to be late.'

'Alright, darling, I'm ready,' Nana walks back to the living room with Dimple. She is a dark-skinned, medium built woman in her mid-sixties. She is wearing a pretty hat and a lemon jumper underneath her black winter coat.

Nana is the senior Mrs Robinson, Mum to Adam and Dimple's dad. She moved from Edinburgh to London a year ago to live with her son after her husband died.

'Let me see your outfit, you look lovely, darling. What character are you in the school play again?'

Dimple gives a quick twirl. 'I am the narrator, Nana. I am in the play from start to finish, so I need to leave this house now!' She pulls Nana to a stop at the staircase.

'Adam! Where are you?' She bellows.

Just then, Adam descends from his bedroom. At 16 years of age, he is almost as tall as his mum.

He towers over his nan and gives her a peck on the cheek. 'You look lovely, Nana.'

Nana beams. 'Thank you, dear. You look more like your dad every day,' She tells him, patting his head.

'I am the cooler version of your son, Nana,' he replies cheekily. Tall and lanky, Adam has short, curly black hair. There is a single plait in the middle of his hair at the back of his head.

'Can you make me a new plait, Dimple?' He asks.

'Are you kidding me?' Dimple grumbles. She is not amused. 'Not now, Adam. I'll do it for you when we get back. That's if we get to school on time at this rate!'

'Dad! What are you still doing up there?' There is no reply.

'Patience, Dimple,' Mum says.' We will make it. Nana, don't forget your shawl.'

'I almost did! Thanks for reminding me.' Nana hurries back to her room.

Dimple sighs again. 'I give up!' She slumps onto the bottom step, then perks up as the strong scent of aftershave wafts towards her. 'You are finally ready,' She says without looking up.

'Who are we waiting for now?' Dad asks, strolling down the carpeted stairs to join the rest of the family. 'I am smartly dressed *and* timely, unlike all of you in this house.' He is wearing a black blazer with a white shirt peeking out underneath. He is not wearing a tie, but still manages to look quite dapper.

Dimple grabs Dad's hand and tugs him towards the door. 'Come along, Dad!' He is 6 feet tall with big, broad shoulders, but he allows himself to be dragged across the living room and hallway.

Dad works in a different hospital to Mum, as an ENT[1] doctor.

---

[1] Ear, Nose and Throat Specialist

Nana returns, and they are finally ready to leave. Dad, Mum and Adam grab their winter coats by the metal hanger just inside the house, and they head out.

It is the end of the rush hour but despite the time of the day, there is heavy traffic and Dad eventually drives into the school gates at 6.50 pm.

'Bye, everyone. Wish me luck!' Dimple says, jumping out of the car before Dad switches off the engine.

'Be careful, young girl!' Nana calls after her.

♦♦♦♦♦♦♦

'Where is Dimple?' Amara asks the rest of the cast backstage.

Just then, Dimple runs in, huffing and puffing. 'Did someone mention my name? I'm here!'

'Dimple, you are late.' Amara says. She looks a little exhausted. 'Miss asked us to get to school thirty minutes before the show starts.'

'Sorry, I couldn't get everyone out of the house,' Dimple replies. 'Ugh! I'm so out of breath.' She looks around the room. 'Are we all here?'

Amara nods.

Just then, Zainab, Natalie, Michael and the other students emerge from the dressing rooms.

Dimple smiles at Michael. 'I hope you've managed to control your nerves?' Michael is Dimple's cousin. He is the youngest of Aunty Nadia's three boys.

Michael smiles nervously back at Dimple. She gives him a reassuring hug, and immediately Michael looks more confident.

The school hall, which usually sits about five hundred chairs, is packed. Dimple's family enter the school hall to take their seats behind Aunty Nadia. Nadia is Mum's younger sister. She also has black, curly hair, but today her hair is in braids.

Mum taps her arm. 'We're here!'

'You finally made it. Nothing ever changes when it comes to your family's time keeping,' Nadia says playfully before smiling at Nana. 'Come sit by my side, Nana.'

'We've made enough disruptions to sit here behind you, but thanks for the offer,' Nana replies, patting her shoulder.

'Hello, Aunty.' David says to Mum. He is a year older than Adam, but they get on very well.

Adam pats his cousins on the back. 'David, Samuel,' He whispers. 'Where is Michael?'

David turns around. 'He is in the school play, too.'

Samuel greets Dad, Mum and Nana.

'How are you doing, young man?' Dad asks him.

'Fine, thanks, Uncle.' Samuel replies. He is the same age as Adam but not as tall. He is sporting a stud gold earring in his left ear.

Dimple and her friends peek out from behind the stage to know the exact spot where their family members are sitting. Dimple waves when she sees Nana and quickly hides back behind the curtains.

The headteacher, Mr Singleton, walks up to the stage, taps on the microphone, and the murmuring dies down.

'Good evening, and welcome to our Christmas play. By the end of the show, I'm sure you'll agree that the children have worked tremendously hard... I will now invite Dimple to the stage,' he concludes.

Dimple walks up to the stage proudly and takes the microphone. This is the moment she has been waiting for. A time to be in the limelight, to shine and show her talent as a natural speaker. She has been rehearsing at home, with Nana as her audience.

'This is the story about the birth of an extraordinary baby boy...' As Dimple begins her narration, the other students file in from behind the stage. She introduces each character, and the play starts.

'Mary, a young teenager from the village of Nazareth, was engaged to be married to Joseph, a Jewish carpenter...'

Forty minutes later, Dimple returns to centre stage. '...And so, despite the unusual beginning and adversity, a child was born in Bethlehem of Judea who will be the saviour of the world. I hope you enjoyed our play! I will now invite the whole cast back to the stage for a final time.'

The cast take a final bow to thunderous applause from their proud parents and other guests.

'That was a good performance by Dimple.' Zainab's mum says as the guests leave the school hall, and the parents reunite with their children.

'All the children did brilliantly,' Dimple's mum replies.

'Agreed. It has been a lovely evening,' Nana concludes.

Dimple joins her brother and the rest of the family in the school corridor, and they walk towards the car park together.

# CHAPTER 2

## HOLIDAY WITH MUM - 'WHAT ARE THE BEST PLACES TO VISIT?'

*February 2020*

The white taxi pulls up in front of the hotel, a white building with imposing double front doors. It is the half-term break, and Mum is taking Dimple on a short vacation to Paphos. Adam has stayed behind at home with Dad, revising for his upcoming GCSE exams.

Dimple gets out from the left side of the car, clutching Ellie, her teddy bear close to her chest in her left hand. Nana Patricia gave Ellie to Dimple on her first birthday.

Mum exits the taxi, too, and they collect their suitcases from the boot of the car.

'Here you go,' Mum says, handing the driver three crisp bank notes.

'I hope you enjoy your stay, Ma'am,' The driver says in English but with a foreign accent. He waits for them to move from the back of the car before driving off on the gravel path. He is soon out of sight.

The hotel porter walks up. 'Welcome to the Grand Hotel.' He says pleasantly, loading their suitcases onto the empty cart.

Mum and Dimple check in at the reception. The receptionist hands them the keys to Room B26, and they take the lift to the second floor, accompanied by the porter. Then, turning left, they walk down the carpeted corridor to Room B26 at the end of the long hall. The porter lugs their suitcases inside the room and leaves them by the door.

Mum thanks him with a generous tip. He returns her smile, gives a short nod and closes the door behind him.

Dimple takes a good look around the room. There are two double beds, a large television in the middle of the room, and a sliding door leading to a tiny terrace. She can see a giant swimming pool and beautiful hills surrounding the town.

She picks the bed next to the sliding doors and opens her pink suitcase. 'I think I'm going to like it here, Mum.'

Mum walks over to watch her unpack. 'How many swimming costumes do you have in your suitcase, Miss?'

'Just my blue one-piece costume, the orange two-piece, and that new purple polka dot swimming suit.'

'Did you say just? Three swimming costumes for a week's holiday?'

'You know I love to swim, Mum. You always say to me "Be prepared", so I came prepared.' She grins and arranges her clothes on three clothes hangers in the closet. 'Here you go, Mum. You can have the rest of the hangers for your clothes.'

'Thank you, Miss Dimple.' Mum says with a smile.

Dimple inspects the rest of the room. A menu, a guide to the hotel facilities and a telephone are on the table next to her bed. The sun is filtering in through the blinds, and she can see the beautiful scenery from her bed.

'You can have your shower first,' Mum says.

Dimple has a shower, and Mum goes into the bathroom after her.

As she is getting dressed, Dimple looks at her watch. 'Mum! We're going to be late! We have only ten minutes left before the hotel restaurant closes for lunch.'

Mum darts into the bedroom, towelling her hair dry.

'I got your blue jeans out with this orange blouse.' Dimple gestures towards Mum's bed and steps out on to the balcony.

'Thanks, darling.' Mum gets dressed quickly and they make their way out of the room. In the lift, she presses the button for the basement where the restaurant is located.

'Room number, please?' The lady at the restaurant desk asks politely. She ticks their room number off the list before guiding them to a table.

*Dimple Dares to Ask*

The restaurant is large but not busy. The room is filled with families, clearly holidaymakers like themselves. From their table, Mum and Dimple can see the sprawling gardens with the trees and the well-manicured lawns.

A waiter appears beside Dimple. 'What would you like to drink?'

'I would like a glass of apple juice, please.' Dimple replies.

Mum examines the wine menu. 'Red wine and some water for me, thanks.'

After ordering the drinks, they get up from their table and walk over to the buffet section. There is a choice of menus from different continents, desserts and fresh fruit, including olives and figs. There is also an ice cream section. Dimple loves strawberry ice cream.

The staff continue clearing the tables nearby.

Dimple and her mother fill their plates with food and return to their table by the window. Mum has lots of fish and seafood on her plate. Dimple went for chicken and chips with a large dollop of tomato ketchup at the side. She munches on her food contentedly, looking at the other families whose children are making loud noises and eating their food simultaneously. Just then, she spots a group of young men dressed in football kits.

'Mum! Mum! Don't look yet, but guess who is here?'

Mum smiles. Her daughter's excitement can be infectious. 'Who?'

'It's the Time Bridge football team!'

'You mean, Adam's Time Bridge football team?'

'Yes! The one and ONLY Adam's Time Bridge Squad!'

'What a coincidence!'

Dimple beams. 'Adam will be very jealous. Remember when he stopped supporting Dad's favourite football club?'

'How can I forget? He was in Year 6. He came home from school one day and said to me,

"Guess what, Mum? I now support the Time Bridge football team." Just like that, I had to change his bedcovers, towel, pyjamas, hat, socks, school bag, mug, everything, to Time Bridge paraphernalia. It cost me a fortune!'

'I remember you told him not to change his mind again.'

'Thank God, he has stayed with them since.'

They finish their meal and as they walk towards the lifts, they see the hotel souvenir shop opposite the restaurant door. They browse through the varied postcards at the entrance before going inside. Inside the shop are t-shirts, postcards, calendars, fridge magnets, sun cream and assorted drinks.

Dimple tries on a pair of sunglasses and a big sun hat, striking a pose for Mum.

'How lovely, darling. The sunglasses are a bit big for you, don't you think?'

'All the models wear big sunglasses these days, Mum.'

'Not for you, young lady.' Mum browses through the rack. 'Look, here's a decent pair for an 11-year-old.'

'Mum! Even Nana won't wear these ones. I'll buy this lovely bracelet instead, if I may?'

Mum nods. Dimple puts the bracelet in a basket and picks a postcard too. She sets it on the counter to write a message to her brother:

*Hey Adam,*

*Paphos is a lovely city. We are in Room B26 on the second floor. We can see the hotel swimming pool from our bedroom balcony. There is so much food! I even had strawberry ice cream for dessert. You would have enjoyed it if you were here.*

*Guess what? The Time Bridge players are staying in this hotel too! How 'sick' is that?*

*Love and kisses to Dad and Nana.*

*See you soon!*

*P.S. – Don't forget to do all your assignments, Adam.* 😊

*Your lovely sister,*

*Dimple xx*

She pays the lady behind the counter for the bracelet, postcard and the postage stamp. The cashier hands her the change and a free map of the city. 'I hope you enjoy your stay.'

'What are the best places to visit?' Mum asks.

'There are several cruises that you can book at the reception desk as well as a trip to Paphos Aphrodite waterpark,' The lady replies. 'A shuttle bus runs from the hotel at scheduled times.'

Mum gives her a grateful smile. 'Thank you, we will certainly look at all the activities available before we choose which ones to book.'

Dimple and Mum walk toward the hotel entrance where they had spotted a post box earlier.

'Look, Mum! The post box is not red like the ones back home!' She drops the postcard in the bright yellow box, and they return to their room.

*Dimple Dares to Ask*

# CHAPTER 3

## THE TIME BRIDGE SQUAD - 'WHAT IS A VIRUS?'

The following morning, Dimple leaps up, puts on her slippers and pulls the blinds to reveal the sun trickling in through the sliding doors.

She stretches with a satisfied yawn. 'What a beautiful day.'

Mum is reading a book in bed. Dimple switches on the television. The female news anchor is talking about a new virus sweeping through Wuhan, China.

'What is a virus, Mum?' Dimple asks.

'A virus is a microscopic organism that reproduces by invading living cells,' Mum replies. 'It can make a person very ill.'

'How sad,' Dimple says before changing the channel. Half an hour later, she gets dressed and heads to the restaurant for breakfast with Mum.

Today, they are among the first to arrive, and they take their seats by the window, looking out to the neat lawns again.

'*Kalimera*,' the lady at the front desk says to them.

'*Kalimera*,' Dimple replies with a smile.

'Oh, your dimple is so pretty!' the lady says.

Dimple thanks her, grinning widely.

'Good morning,' Mum says at the same time.

Shortly afterwards, the football team arrive, and everyone in the restaurant stares as they take their seats in the corner of the room. There are about eight or nine of them in the group. Dimple looks up at them, pinching herself to make sure it is real. She is having breakfast with the Time Bridge Squad!

She spots Adam's favourite player, Marcus, wearing a white jersey shirt engraved with the number 11 and navy-blue pants. Marcus, a friendly-looking footballer, is very tall, with black curly hair and visible tattoos on his left hand. He sits in the middle of the group, facing the entrance, with his back to Mum and Dimple. He is chatting to his teammates, who are all wearing white jerseys, each with a different number at the back.

After a few minutes, Dimple approaches Marcus and introduces herself. 'My brother is a big fan of Time Bridge, and you are his favourite player.' She tells him. 'Would you sign an autograph for him, please? He couldn't come on holiday with us because he is preparing for his GCSE exams.'

'Of course,' Marcus replies. 'What is your brother's name?'

'Adam.'

'Okay, I will bring a signed photograph for Adam at dinner time.' Marcus promises.

Dimple happily returns to sit with Mum, who is already tucking into a full English breakfast.

'I'm proud of you for being so brave, Dimple.' Mum says.

After the lovely breakfast, Dimple and Mum walk out of the restaurant and head off to sit by the outdoor pool. Mum takes out her sunglasses from her bag and sits on a deck, under a canopy. She starts reading her magazine with a satisfied sigh. Since January, she's been looking forward to this moment when she can finally switch off from everything.

Dimple sits on a blanket by Mum's feet, gazing at the deep blue water in the swimming pool. The pool is surrounded by trees and decks on either side. The view is even more beautiful closeup than when she saw it from their bedroom window.

Mum looks up from her magazine. 'What do you plan to do now, darling?'

'FaceTime Dad.' Dimple replies. 'Then I'm going to read about the virus on my tablet. I want to find out more about it.'

Dimple makes a video call to Dad. He is still in bed because London is two hours behind Paphos. 'Hi, Dad. We've just had the best breakfast, and we are having a rest by the pool.' She rattles away. 'Have you heard about the virus in London, Dad? The one from China?'

'Yes. It's all over the papers and on the news, too.' Dad replies. 'Is it the same over there?'

'Yes. It is so scary, Dad. Oh, I should say, "*Nai*, Daddy". *Nai* means "Yes" in Paphos, you see.'

Dad laughs. 'That sounds like "No" in English. Give the tablet to your Mum, Sweetie.'

Dimple hands the tablet to Mum.

'Hi, love.' Dad says to Mum. 'Please look after yourselves. This virus is nothing like we've ever seen or heard of.'

Dimple peeks around Mum's shoulder. 'Dad, is Adam up yet?'

'Not yet. We all know it's too early for your brother to be awake.'

'Ok, Dad, say hello to Adam.'

'Give our love to Nana.' Mum adds.

Dimple waves him goodbye, then she continues to google the virus on her tablet.

# CHAPTER 4

## A PRESENT FOR DIMPLE – 'WHERE IS THE TIME BRIDGE SQUAD?'

The next day, Mum and Dimple decide to skip breakfast. The short break will be over soon, and they plan to see a little of the town.

'Mind the cobbles,' Mum says to Dimple as they walk up the hill, keeping to the left side of the road.

A car races past. Dimple coughs slightly and waves both arms to get rid of the dust behind the car. 'There is so much dust around,' She mutters before pointing to a building to their right. 'Look, Mum! It's an international school for British students.'

They continue along the road, taking in the surrounding views.

'I'm looking forward to the Aphrodite waterpark trip tomorrow!' Dimple announces.

'You have to wake up early for breakfast before we go,' Mum tells her.

But Dimple doesn't mind that. After about fifteen minutes, they see a large mall to the left side of the road. They go through the shops, looking for presents for the rest of the family.

'What do you think Nana will like?' Dimple asks Mum.

'You could get her a hat. You know Nana loves her hats and scarves.'

They walk into a shop and Dimple picks a sun hat. 'Will Nana like this?'

'Of course, darling. That is a very good choice.'

Mum pays for the hat, and they continue walking through the shops. Then Dimple stops. 'I'm hungry, Mum. Can we get something to eat?'

'There's a café over there.' Mum says. 'Let's see what's on their menu.'

They walk towards the café, a brown hut with the roof made from raffia. There is a small white board with a handwritten menu. A couple of diners are sitting at the tables set outside, drinking and chatting. The tables are covered with embroidered tablecloths and table mats made from raffia.

The aroma of coffee greets Dimple and Mum as they enter the hut. Chairs are set behind round tables on either side of the café. Behind the till is a board with the menu and prices.

Dressed in brown uniforms with green aprons, the staff are busy taking orders, making tea and coffee, colliding occasionally as they try to serve the customers.

Mum and Dimple take their seats.

'I could eat a horse!' Dimple announces. 'But I will have some croissants with a cup of tea, please, Mum.'

Mum goes over to the young man behind the counter. 'I'll have two croissants with one tea and one coffee, please.'

'Any sugar?'

'*Nai*,' Mum says. Dimple grins at Mum's attempt to speak the local language.

The food is soon served and Dimple munches happily. 'This croissant is hot and delicious.'

Mum sips her drink. 'The coffee is excellent too.'

'I'm tired now,' Dimple says, after they've eaten. 'Can we take a taxi back to the hotel, please?'

Mum agrees and a taxi soon stops in front of their hotel. An exhausted Dimple has slept through the five-minute journey.

'Excuse me. You have a parcel at the reception desk,' The porter says to Mum as they enter the hotel.

'Oh, I wonder who it's from,' Mum says, making her way to the reception desk. The hotel reception is not busy at all, but there is a small queue of people waiting to check out.

They wait until a receptionist is free. 'Is there a parcel for me please?' Mum asks when it's their turn.

The receptionist asks for their room number.

'We're in B26,' Mum replies.

'One moment. Let me check. Ah, there is something here for Miss Dimple.'

Dimple is puzzled. 'For me?'

The lady hands her a small parcel.

'Thank you,' Dimple says politely. They take the lift to their bedroom. Once inside, Dimple opens the parcel excitedly.

'Oh, it's the signed photograph from Marcus.'

'There is a note attached.' Mum points out, looking over Dimple's shoulder.

> *'Dear Dimple,*
>
> *Please give this signed photograph and football shirt to Adam. We had to leave early this morning because two of our players suddenly fell sick. The tournament is cancelled.*
>
> *Take care of yourself and have a safe flight home.*
>
> *Best wishes,*
>
> *Marcus'*

'Oh, that's an awful thing to happen,' Mum says.

Dimple sighs. 'It's a shame that I didn't get to see Marcus before they left. I hope they get better soon.' She grabs her tablet and facetimes her brother.

*A Present for Dimple – 'Where is The Time Bridge Squad?'*

'Hi Adam. The Time Bridge Squad left early after the tournament got cancelled. But Marcus left you a signed photograph.'

Adam asks her what happened.

'Some players fell ill.'

'That's unfortunate. But thanks for getting the autograph. Marcus is the GOAT, 'Greatest of All Times,'' Adam is saying when the room telephone rings.

Mum picks it up. 'Room B26.'

'Hello Mrs Robinson, it's Heidi from the reception desk. I'm afraid tomorrow's scheduled trip to the waterpark is cancelled.'

'Why is that?' Mum enquires.

'Government advice, because of the virus. We are monitoring the situation, but we felt it best not to continue with the tour. The tour operators will refund your money in full.'

'By the way, do you know why the football team left early?'

'A couple of the players developed a high temperature, and the goalkeeper kept coughing. They were treated at the local hospital, but the coach decided to call off the game to protect everyone else.'

Mum thanks her before putting the phone back on the table. Dimple hangs up on her brother at the same time.

'Oh no!' She says glumly after Mum gives her the news. 'I was looking forward to the waterpark tour.'

'We'd better get ready for dinner.' Mum tells her.

*Dimple Dares to Ask*

# CHAPTER 5

## RETURNING HOME -
## 'HOW LONG IS OUR FLIGHT?'

'Passports, please.' The lady in the smart red uniform at the airport desk says to Dimple and her mum. The holiday is over, and it is time to go back home.

Mum hands over both passports.

The smartly dressed lady scans their passports and returns them to Mum. 'I hope you enjoyed your stay and do have a safe flight.'

'How long is our flight, please?' Dimple asks. She is anxious to get back to Dad and Adam.

'The flight from Paphos to the United Kingdom takes four hours and forty-six minutes,' The lady replies.

They board the plane and Dimple takes the window seat. Mum covers her legs with the blanket.

'Thanks, Mum.' She glances at her watch. 'We should be home by 7pm.'

'Don't forget the airport checks and the journey home as well.'

As the flight soars in the air, Dimple thinks of the few places they visited on her holiday. She wishes she had seen the Paphos Aphrodite water park. She will miss the swimming pool and the menu.

'At least I got the signed autograph for Adam.' She says to Mum who is reading an inflight magazine.

The flight attendant stops beside their seat with the meal trolley.

'Chicken, beef or vegetables?'

'Chicken please,' Dimple announces. 'It's my favourite.'

'I'll have the beef,' Mum replies.

Once the food is served, Dimple stashes the bread roll in her bag. 'I'm taking it home for Adam,' She explains to Mum. After her meal, she starts watching a film but soon falls into a deep sleep. Before she knows it, the pilot is giving instructions over the tannoy.

'Please return to your seats, fasten your seat belts and prepare for landing.'

The plane touches the ground with a mighty thud, followed by a screeching noise. Dimple covers her ears with both hands. A few minutes later, they are approaching the self-checking E-Gates.

Dimple goes first. She places her passport on the reader, smiles at the camera and walks through to wait for Mum on the other side. They walk towards the exit where Adam and Dad are waiting. Dimple bounds up to them and leaps into Dad's arms.

'Dad! Did you miss me?'

'Of course, I did, Princess.' Dad gives her a kiss. 'How was your flight, and did you have a lovely holiday?'

'Hi, Mum.' Adam says, planting a kiss on Mum's cheek.

Mum pats his cheeks. 'Hello, darling. Has Dad been feeding you? I can see your cheekbones.'

Adam's eyes twinkle. 'Of course, he has.'

'Yeah, Yeah, blame everything on Dad.' Dad quips. 'We all know who the best cook in the house is!'

On the way home, Dimple talks excitedly about everything she saw on holiday with Mum, and soon they are back in their modest home. Nana opens the door, smiling from cheek to cheek.

'Hello, Nana!' Dimple blurts out. 'Guess what I brought back for you?'

'Let me guess: some lovely diamonds?'

'I'm not that rich, Nana, at least not yet. Wait till I graduate from University.' Dimple unzips her suitcase. 'I bought you a sun hat. It's made of straw with a yellow ribbon, your favourite colour.'

Nana examines the hat with a huge smile. 'Thank you, my darling. It's lovely.'

Dimple drags her luggage upstairs to her bedroom.

Dad switches on the television. The news reader is talking about the virus again. It is now sweeping through other countries across the continents. Just then, Dimple walks back into the living room.

'We heard this story in Paphos.' She says. 'I want this virus to go away!'

Changing the subject, Mum turns to Nana Patricia. 'Did you keep well while we were away?'

'No complaints. Just the usual aches and pains. Thank you.'

Everyone settles in as Dimple hands out presents to Dad and Adam, regaling them with her holiday stories until dinnertime.

♦♦♦♦♦♦♦

Dimple goes to bed, still thinking of the virus. She is also looking forward to school the next day when she will see all her friends again.

'I can't wait to tell them all about my holiday…' She whispers before falling asleep with Ellie beside her.

# CHAPTER 6

## NANA PLAYS THE PIANO FOR HER FRIENDS – 'WHAT IS LOCKDOWN?'

*March 2020*

Nana is sitting at the head of the six-seater dining table, with Adam and Dimple on each side of her. They are having breakfast to start off the day. Mum enters with a plate. 'Here's some more toast if anyone wants more.'

Adam looks up. 'Thanks, Mum. May I have some more omelette, please?'

'Sure.' Mum scoops up the remaining eggs into a bowl and hands it over. 'Hurry up, you two, or you'll be late for school. Nana, when you are ready, I can drop you off at the club on my way to work. I start slightly later today.'

Nana attends the local over 60's club on Wednesdays and Fridays.

'Yes, please. That would be great.' Nana wipes her mouth with a tea towel.

Dad comes down and makes himself a cup of coffee. 'Morning, everyone.'

'Are you not going to eat, Son?' Nana asks.

Dad straightens his tie. 'I have an early meeting today. I'll be late if I don't leave now.'

Adam scoffs the rest of his food, dashes upstairs and returns with his school bag. He gives his mum a peck on the cheek. 'I'm off. See you later. Bye Nana!' he yells before closing the front door behind him.

Dad looks at Dimple. 'Why are you still sitting at the dining table, young lady? Would you like a lift to school?'

Dimple takes her plate to the kitchen and places it in the sink. 'It's okay. I'm going with Natalie, Zainab and Amara. Natalie's mum is driving us to school today.' She heads for the living room. 'I'm just leaving now. I'll get my bag and walk outside with you, Dad.'

Dad kisses Mum on the cheek. 'Bye, love. Bye, Nana!' He and Dimple head out.

Mum sits down with a cup of coffee and a slice of toast with marmalade. 'I've peeled the potatoes and prepared the vegetables for dinner later.' She tells Nana.

'That's kind of you, Dear. What are we having?'

'Boiled or mashed potatoes. Whichever you prefer.'

'That sounds great. Okay, I'll go and get ready.' Nana walks to her room on the ground floor.

*Nana plays the piano for her friends – 'What is Lockdown?'*

'I'll get dressed in a mo.' Mum clears the table and goes upstairs to get ready. When she gets back downstairs, Nana is still getting dressed.

'Ready, Nana?'

Nana exits her bedroom looking lovely in her cream blouse and brown skirt. 'Yes, dear. Let's go.' They grab their coats and step out into the brisk cold morning. Nana soon settles into the passenger seat. Just as Mum prepares to drive away, the nine o'clock news comes on the radio:

'The Covid-19 virus is the biggest threat this country has faced for decades,' The news reader says.

'Do you understand this virus, Gloria?' Nana asks.

'Just what I've heard on the news so far, Nana.' Gloria replies mildly, navigating on to the main road leading to the club. She does not want to scare Nana with the grim details surrounding the virus. 'We are learning more about the symptoms with each day,' she continues.

'I hope they find a cure very soon,' Nana says, offering a quick silent prayer.

Gloria pulls up outside the club. The Over 60's Social club is a red, brick bungalow on the High Street. There is parking for up to six cars in front of the building. The main door is black and can be seen as you drive into the compound. Blue, white, red, pink, and purple sunflowers are on both sides of the entrance.

Mum pulls up outside. 'There you are, Nana. I will see you at home in the evening.'

Nana steps out of the car. 'Thanks, Gloria.' She waves and makes her way in.

Her friend John approaches her at the entrance. 'Hello, Pat.'

'How are you, John?'

'I'm fine,' He says, 'but you will make my day if you have the first dance with me today.'

Nana chuckles. 'Only if you promise not to step on my toes.'

They enter the wide main hall. The room is bright, with the sun seeping in through the open windows. Tables and chairs are arranged in circles across the floor. There are beautiful flowers in tall glass vases on each table, and a piano sits at the far right of the room next to a central stage. An arch made from balloons is at the top of the stage.

'Where are the others?' Nana asks. 'Hello Mable, how are you keeping? Is Rhona not in today?'

'Very well, thanks, Pat,' Mable says. 'I haven't seen Rhona yet. Perhaps we can go home together today if that's alright with you?'

'Of course! I look forward to going home with you as always, Mable.'

The over 60s members club is a small community of about twenty local residents. They are a diverse group - John and Mable are White British, Sally is from Zimbabwe and Nana is of a mixed Caribbean heritage. Other members of the club are from the Philippines and the Seychelles. Occasionally, members invite their friends and families to join them.

Nana, John and Mable sit at the same table. The other three tables in the hall are all occupied by men and women chatting to each other. Once the ladies stash away their coats and bags, John leads the way to the buffet. They all select from the sandwiches and fruits and return to their seats. Soon they are playing games and chatting with each other across the room.

'Sally? Are you not eating?' John asks a pale lady in her seventies sitting quietly at the table to their right.

Sally looks at him blankly. 'I have no appetite these days. I seem to have lost my sense of taste as well.'

'But the coffee smells great!' Nana interjects. 'You should try some.'

'I can't even smell that,' Sally replies. 'I'll just have some hot water with lemon.'

John gets up. 'I'll get that ordered for you.' He marches off. The ladies exchange smiles. John is so good at looking after them all.

Mable takes out her knitting kit and shows Nana the shawl she is making.

'That's exquisite,' Nana exclaims. 'Why don't you sell them? You would make a tidy sum. You are really talented.'

'I only knit to keep myself busy,' Mable replies with a soft smile. She is a quiet woman who has gifted Nana with shawls of different colours ever since they met three years ago.

'I still have the blue shawl you gave me last Christmas,' Nana tells her. 'It's lovely and warm.'

Just then, John returns with Sally's hot water, and a slow song comes on. He places the glass in front of Sally and turns to Nana with a smile. 'You promised me the first dance, Pat!'

'Alright then.' Nana rises to her feet, and they begin to dance.

John holds her right hand and places his other arm around her waist. As they start swaying to the music, other couples join them on the dance floor. The next song is much faster, and even more couples fill the dance floor, conversing, smiling and singing along to the lyrics.

Nana and John return to their table a little later to find Mable staring into her glass. Nana can tell she hasn't taken a sip.

*What's wrong with her?* John whispers. Pat shrugs and steps forward to sit next to Mable. She glances around and sees that Sally has already left.

'What's on your mind, Mable? You look pensive and your tea has clearly gone cold.'

Mable looks up and shakes her head. 'Has anyone heard of the coronavirus?'

'I was discussing it with my daughter-in-law. You know she is a nurse,' Nana replies, relaxing into her seat. 'She doesn't know too much about it yet.'

'It's in the news a lot,' John says. 'It originated from Wuhan, China, if I'm correct.'

Nana nods.

'I really hope the government nips it in the bud before it spreads over here.' Mable says, looking distinctly worried.

Nana takes a deep breath, marches across to the piano at the corner of the room and begins to play a tune. Mable moves over to stand next to her and starts singing in a soft voice:

*'There will be bluebirds over the white cliffs of Dover...*

*There will be peace and laughter*[2]*...*

The music playing from the speakers tails off and the other dancers return to their seats. Everyone stops talking to watch. The song finishes and a round of applause follows Nana and Mable to their table. Nana gets her glasses case out of her handbag and reinserts the reading glasses she wore when playing the piano.

The club's activities start in earnest, and everyone is having a wonderful time. A little while later, Nana looks at her watch.

'Oh, I have to leave now,' she tells John. 'My daughter-in-law is working a late shift today, so I offered to help James with the dinner.'

---

[2] (There'll Be Bluebirds Over) The White Cliffs of Dover; Words by Nat Burton and Music by Walter Kent (1941–42)

'That's kind of you.' John says, grabbing his glass.

'It's the least I can do. Gloria kindly dropped me here this morning. God knows when she will get back tonight, if at all. She has been working double shifts to help with the shortage of staff at the hospital.'

Nana waves good-bye to those who are still dancing and chatting to each other. Mable materialises beside her.

'Give me one sec.' John finishes his drink in one gulp and gets to his feet. 'I'll walk you and Mable to the bus stop.'

'Are you ready, Mable?' Nana asks.

'I'll just get my bag.' Mable says. She takes her Freedom Pass[3] out of the handbag. 'All good to go.'

They walk the short distance to the bus-stop. Mable sits on one of the orange seats at the bus terminal, while Nana stands, talking to John. The weather is slightly breezy, and Nana wraps her scarf tightly around her neck. She is wearing a light brown coat. Mable's coat is similar but black.

Just then, they see the 64-bus approaching.

'See you same time next week, then?' John says to Nana.

'By God's grace,' Nana replies, getting out her own Freedom Pass. 'I will start thinking of the songs to play next week after dinner tonight.'

---

[3] The Freedom Pass allows anyone over 60 to ride for free on public transport at certain times of the day.

'I'm sure you will come up with something, Pat.' John says. 'You always do.' He waits until the ladies are seated, waves and heads off in the other direction. Three stops later, they get off, and Nana walks Mable to her door before going home.

As she opens the front door to the house, the aroma of grilled sausages and herbs wafts in her direction. Dad puts his head out of the kitchen door. He is wearing a blue apron. Adam is standing behind him. Nana sets her bag down on the centre table and walks over to them.

'Hello, Nana, How was your day?' Dad calls her Nana like everyone else in the family.

'Very good, thanks. They have introduced computing lessons at the club, which I enjoyed. Thanks to you, Adam, I did much better than some of the others. Then, I came home with Mable as usual.'

'That's great, Nana!' Adam teases with a smile. 'Soon I won't have to help you with emails and text messages.'

Nana pats his shoulder. 'We'll have to see how I get on with the lessons.'

'I'm sure you'll do well.' Dad says confidently.

'Yep. We'll soon be calling Nana, "Nana Microsoft."' Adam adds.

'Nana, don't mind Daddy and Adam.' Nana looks up to see Dimple coming down the stairs. 'I can share my IT notes with you, and you can ask me questions.'

'Hello, Darling.' Nana says, smiling. 'How was your day at school?'

'School was a bit quiet,' Dimple replies, frowning slightly.

'You look troubled.' Nana says. 'What's wrong?'

'Many of my friends weren't at school today. Quite a few classes had absent students and teachers. I wonder what's going on.'

Nana reaches down and gives her a hug. 'Don't worry about it, Dimple. Everything will be fine.' She picks up her bag. 'I'll just have a quick shower before dinner.' As she heads to her room, she recalls the conversation with John and Mable at the club. The situation is becoming rather worrying.

Dimple switches on the television before joining Dad and Adam in the kitchen. 'What's for dinner, Dad?'

'Mashed potatoes with sausage, gravy and vegetables.'

She heads for the cutlery drawer. 'I'll set the table.'

'I'll just go and charge my phone in my room,' Adam says as soon as Dimple opens the drawer.

'Typical!' Dimple huffs. 'As soon as I come downstairs, you rush off to avoid doing any work.'

Adam scuttles out of the kitchen. 'I'll be back in a jiffy. My battery has gone really low.'

Dimple sets down the cutlery. 'Dad! You didn't say anything to Adam. He's always skiving, to avoid doing any work in the house.'

'Be fair to your brother, Dimple. He prepared all the vegetables and washed the breakfast dishes before you came down.'

'No,' Dimple says firmly. '*Mum* peeled the potatoes and prepared the vegetables earlier.'

'Okay. He washed the breakfast dishes at least.' Dad replies, ladling the food into the dishes and setting them down on the dining table.

'Yeah right,' Dimple says, unimpressed. 'I'll bet he didn't wash the dishes, either.'

Nana returns, and they all sit at the table. At that precise moment, Adam joins them.

His sister gives him a knowing look. 'Welcome back, Adam.'

Dimple says The Grace, and they start to eat.

'What time does Gloria finish her shift today?' Nana asks Dad.

'She's working until 11pm.'

Just then, the caption at the bottom of the television screen flashes. *Prime Minister announces Lockdown.*'

Dimple eyes the screen for a moment, then turns to Dad. 'What's a Lockdown?'

'It is when the government imposes strict restrictions on travel, mingling with others, and access to public places.' Dad replies. He now looks concerned. 'From what I understand, we are not allowed to go out unnecessarily or visit others.'

The Prime Minister is speaking:

*'Good Evening. The coronavirus is the biggest threat this country has faced for decades – and this country is not alone. All over the world we are seeing the devastating impact of this invisible killer...And so tonight I want to update you on the latest steps we are taking to fight the disease and what you can do to help... It's vital to slow the spread of the disease... reduce the number of people needing hospital treatment...and save more lives. That's why we have been asking people to stay at home during this pandemic.*

*And though huge numbers are complying...From this evening, you **must** stay at home...People will only be allowed to leave their home for the following very limited purposes: shopping for basic necessities, one form of exercise a day, to provide care or to help a vulnerable person; and travelling to and from work, but only where this is absolutely necessary and cannot be done from home.'*

The family exchange amazed looks as he announces the closure of all shops selling non-essential goods and bans gatherings of more than two people and all social events excluding funerals.

Dimple doesn't know how to feel.

Several minutes later, he concludes... *'We will come through it stronger than ever. We will beat the coronavirus and we will beat it together...at this moment of national emergency, stay at home, protect our NHS and save lives. Thank you*[4].'

The Robinsons eat the rest of their meal in stunned silence.

---

[4] Published 23 March 2020
Source - (Gov.UK)

*Dimple Dares to Ask*

# CHAPTER 7

## CLAP FOR THE NHS AND OUR CARERS - 'WHERE IS EVERYONE TONIGHT?'

***April 2020***

'Anyone at home?' Dad yells as he enters the house after a hard day at the hospital. The time is 7:50 pm on a Thursday evening.

Dimple runs excitedly from her room two stairs at a time to greet Dad with a big hug and kiss. 'Mwah! Welcome home, Dad.'

'Careful, love. I've warned you to come down one stair at a time. You'll fall over and hurt yourself one of these days.'

'I'm okay, Dad. I was just so happy to see you.' Dimple is bouncing up and down. It's her favourite day of the week.

'Where's everyone else? I thought you would all be outside, getting ready to clap for the NHS.'

'Mum and Nana are in the garden,' Dimple reports, sounding a little frustrated. 'They say they are on their way, but I think they are enjoying the evening sunshine a little too much.'

She links her arm through Dad's, and they head past the kitchen to the glass patio door that leads to the conservatory through to the garden. The garden is a moderate size, around which Mum has planted some red roses, dandelions, fuchsia and gerbera daisies. Nana also has a small plot at the bottom of the garden where she grows tomatoes, cucumbers and sweetcorn in different patches.

A table covered by a huge black and white parasol is in the middle of the garden. Mum and Nana are relaxing in the bright sunlight on two of its four chairs.

Mum looks up and smiles when she sees Dad. She rises and gives him a peck on the cheek. 'I know, I know,' she says, laughing at her daughter's slightly miffed expression. 'Let me get my shawl.'

Adam comes into the garden. 'Hi, Dad. I was just finishing a game on my computer.'

They troop over to the front of the house through the back gate. Across the street and around them, doors open, and their neighbours pour out to stand outside their houses. At the stroke of 8pm, a loud cheer erupts, and everyone starts clapping. Others join in from their window sills.

In the middle of the road, Shakira leads a small group of boys and girls in a dance routine. Every child on the street aged between four and sixteen is welcome to join in. Dimple runs across.

'Hi Shakira,' She inserts herself in between Amber and Toby from No. 12.

'Right, watch my steps everyone and repeat my moves,' Shakira shouts.

*Left, left, slide*
*Back to back*
*Right slide*
*Then turn around*
*Two steps slide*
*Two steps slide*

Other neighbours are banging their pots with big spoons through their bedroom windows, in time with the dancing children, creating distinctive rhythmic sounds. Dimple looks forward to this community act every week. It is the highlight of Lockdown.

Dad is talking to Franklin across the fence. 'Funny how we live next door but hardly see each other except when we come out to clap for the NHS.'

'I'll say, James,' Franklin says. 'It has taken the pandemic to make us aware of the sacrifices our key workers make to keep this country going. You and your lovely wife included, of course!'

Dad chuckles. 'Thanks. We shouldn't forget the postal workers too. Bob delivers our letters every day, come rain or shine.'

Franklin nods vigorously. 'That he does. I have even received letters at 9pm on a Saturday evening or early Sunday morning.

'They are all our heroes,' Dad concludes. A barking sound makes him peep over the fence. 'What's that by your side?'

'Oh, that's Terry, my new corgi,' Franklin replies. 'I got a puppy to keep me company now that I'm working from home. She keeps me fit, I tell you. Although, I don't know what'll happen to our morning walks when I return to work.'

Dad admires the cute little black and white puppy from a distance. 'The lockdown has been difficult for people who live alone,' he says, 'and many have relied on and probably would not have survived without their four-legged friends for companionship.'

Franklin leans down to pick up the puppy. 'It is true what they say. "A dog is not just for Christmas, but for life." What happens to our pets after lockdown remains to be seen.'

'Do you know when you are going back to the office?'

'Not yet. It will be a hybrid of office and home working, which will allow me to continue with my morning exercises with this little one,' Franklin replies as he strokes her head with affection.

# CHAPTER 8

## LEARNING AWAY FROM SCHOOL – 'WHY IS THE INTERNET CONNECTION SLOW?'

***June 2020***

It has been three months since the prime minister's announcement in March. No one is allowed to travel around, schools are shut, and workers have been told to work from home where possible.

The last two terms of primary school are challenging for Dimple. She is home schooling, and all her assignments are online. During the first few weeks, she struggles to use 'Microsoft Teams' and other online platforms. Every class is online, and she has different subjects each day. Sometimes the online photos she needs for assignments are grainy. She also has to print every word document and put them in folders. Dimple eventually adapts to the different routine of attending classes online. However, the teachers set her work without interactions, and she does not feel she is learning as much as when she went to school.

Tonight, Dimple is in her bedroom, which is the third to the right along the corridor on the top floor. The little light coming into the room reflects on the mirror opposite Dimple's white wardrobe. Next to her bed, there is a single chair and a table. Her laptop is connected to a white monitor. At the back of her room, there is a two-shelf bookcase. On the top shelf, there are novels and magazines. Her schoolbooks and files are at the bottom.

The alarm clock on the windowsill goes off a second time, but Dimple is chatting with Zainab on Microsoft Teams.

'I like the colour of your wallpaper.' Zainab says. 'It's new, isn't it?'

'Yes, it's my favourite colour! Mum has been doing some DIY and I asked her to change the pink wallpaper to lilac.'

'Lucky you, I still have the same ABC wallpaper from when I was a baby!' Zainab says enviously, craning her neck to see the magazine cut outs of famous catwalk models in gorgeous dresses pasted around the room. She spots the big, coloured poster opposite Dimple's bed.

'Gosh! Where did you get that nice poster of Justin Bieber?'

'Oh, Adam bought it for me online. I was really surprised since he hardly buys me anything!'

'You're so lucky to have a big brother who is super cool,' Zainab coos.

'I guess so, but it doesn't feel like that whenever he dodges housework. Dad and Nana always cover up for him, and I don't know why.'

'He has a lot of schoolwork, I guess,' Zainab points out. 'Even I am struggling with all the work Miss gives us. I can't keep up!'

'I feel as though I'm in a lecture room instead of school,' Dimple moans. 'Miss doesn't explain the work, and she sets more assignments before we finish the previous ones.'

'I know,' Zainab says. 'I asked a question about the geography assignment, but she has not replied to my email. Now she has given us a history assignment as well?'

Dimple adds their other friends into the chat. 'Let's see what Natalie and Amara think.'

Amara's profile picture shows up. 'Hey, you two. What's going on?' A moment later, her bright smile lights up the screen.

'Hi, Amara. What do you think of the new history assignment?' Dimple asks.

Amara's smile fades and she starts frowning. 'What history assignment? Miss gave us a geography assignment which I have not even started.'

Dimple and Zainab start laughing. 'Amara, have you checked your coursework online?' Zainab finally says.

'The assignment was given two days ago, and it is due at the end of this week.'

Amara reaches for her school folder. 'Oh dear, I'll check now.'

'Should I phone Natalie? She hasn't joined the chat yet.' Just as Zainab reaches for her phone, an exasperated-looking Natalie joins the group.

'Sorry girls, I was looking for a quiet corner before logging in. Rachel and Rochelle are making a racket as usual. Yesterday, I had to lock myself in the toilet downstairs to start my geography assignment. I could do with some peace and quiet in this house!'

'Your twin sisters are adorable,' Dimple says.

'Shall I send them to your house?' Natalie asks in a slightly sarcastic tone.

Dimple smiles. 'Not now, but they are always welcome at our place.'

'Ha-ha! You're only saying that because we're in lockdown,' Natalie replies. 'Cute is the last thing you'd call them if they spent even half a day at your house.'

'Amara has not seen the history assignment,' Zainab tells Natalie.

'I'm looking at it now,' Amara pipes up in a distressed voice. 'Oh dear, I have a lot of catching up to do.'

Natalie sighs. 'Miss keeps throwing assignments at us during this lockdown.'

The friends nod miserably.

Amara is scanning through her notes. 'When is the history assignment due?'

'Thursday,' Zainab replies.

Mum shouts up the stairs. 'Dimple! Are you in your room? Are you chatting to your friends again?' She opens the door.

'We're discussing our school assignments, Mum,' Dimple replies. 'Sorry girls, I have to go now. Catch you later!' She signs off hurriedly.

'The ink in the printer is gone again!' Mum says, looking harassed. Apart from Nana, the whole family looks like that a lot at different times these days.

'I'm not the only person using the printer, Mum!' Dimple exclaims. 'Dad and Adam print more stuff than I do.'

Mum throws her another glance before stalking out of the room. Dimple sighs and returns to her laptop.

♦♦♦♦♦♦♦

For her history assignment, Dimple has been creating a quiz on a slide deck with ten flags from the commonwealth countries. Her bubble[5] peers must

---

[5] An unofficial term describing a cluster of people outside households with whom people were comfortable spending time during the pandemic.

identify which flag belongs to which country, earning a bonus point if they can name the country's leader.

The home internet is not steady, and every task she tries to do runs at a snail's pace. She knows Dad is working on a corporate NHS project and Adam is playing a game on his computer. The demand for the internet is reducing their online access.

'This Wi-Fi connection keeps starting and stopping,' Dimple mutters to herself. On cue, the internet cuts off again. But this time, she has not saved the deck, and she loses the work she has spent so much time on.

'This is the second time this week. It's so frustrating!' She grumbles through gritted teeth. 'Adam! Will you STOP playing your computer games? I need the internet for my assignment!'

There is no reply from her brother's room.

'Adaaaam!!'

Dimple stomps over to Dad's study. 'Dad!'

Dad jumps slightly in his chair.

'Please tell Adam to play his games at night. AFTER I have finished my schoolwork!'

'You know he is not allowed to play games in his room at night,' Dad says. 'What has he done now?'

She flops on the floor. 'He's been at it for hours! Now the internet has disconnected, and I have lost all my work. This history quiz counts towards my year-end assessment. The internet came back on briefly, but I have to start all over again!'

'That's not true!' Adam hollers from his room. 'I only started a few minutes ago.'

'That is a big fat lie, Adam Robinson!' Dimple yells, rushing to her brother's room. 'Tell the truth and let the devil be ashamed!'

'Alright, both of you pack it in!' Dad interjects. 'Dimple, save your work on a memory stick when you start again. In the meantime, I will find out what's gone wrong.'

Dad removes the cables from the socket and plugs them back in again. The internet connection is still not back on, so he calls the broadband provider. A man with a Scottish accent takes Dad through some security questions.

'Please confirm your name and the first line of your address.'

'James Robinson – 25 The Coppins, SW11 xxx'

'Thank you. How may I help you today, Mr Robinson?'

'We lost our internet connection about half an hour ago, while my daughter was working on her school assignment.'

'Have you tried removing the cables and plugging them back in?'

'I did that, but there has been no change.'

'We'll check that the fault is not from our end, Mr Robinson.'

After what seems like an eternity, the connectivity is restored, and Dimple returns to her room to complete her assignment.

'Are you the only student in the country?' Adam teases her from across the hallway. 'It's the end of the school year. You need to chill, Little Sis!'

'That's easy for you to say, Adam,' Dimple says huffily. 'Mum and Dad have promised me a treat if I get the best academic report for the year.'

Adam laughs. 'Princess Perfect,' he says, before shutting his bedroom door.

# CHAPTER 9

## MUM AT WORK - 'WHERE ARE THE FAMILY MEMBERS?'

*May 2020*

Dad is driving Mum on Saturday morning to the hospital where she works as an anaesthetic nurse. The hospital, located at the end of Lodge Lane, off Bickley Road, is usually a 45-minute drive from home. Dad turns right into Bickley road, but the street ahead is busy. Mum's shift started at 5am and the time is now 5:10, even though they left home at four.

'Why is there so much traffic around Lodge Lane?' Mum asks.

'Beats me,' Dad replies. 'It's unusual for this time of the day. And why are so many ambulances queuing at the hospital gates?'

'This is becoming a common trend since the outbreak of Coronavirus,' Mum replies. 'Last week, the hospital ran out of oxygen supply.'

'It's the same scenario at my hospital,' Dad points out. 'Did you remember to take your visor?'

'I did. Thanks, love,' Mum replies. 'Dimple asked me what a visor was, the other day, and I had to explain that a visor is a transparent headgear that protects the face and eyes. Who would ever have expected masks and visors to become part of commonplace conversations?' She chuckles briefly, then continues on a more serious note. 'We've also had a shortage of PPE[6]. But despite this and staff shortages, the doctors and medical staff are working hard, and patients are getting better and going home.'

'This wave of the virus is severe, love,' Dad says, just as they arrive at the hospital's front entrance.

Mum grabs her bag from the passenger seat. 'Yes, the symptoms are unpredictable and differ from patient to patient. The mental stress on our medical team is horrendous.' With a sigh, she gives Dad a quick kiss and steps out of the car. 'Drive home safely.'

♦♦♦♦♦♦♦

Dr Patel greets Mum as she enters the ward. 'Morning Gloria.' He is wearing a face mask, a visor, an apron, and protective gloves. A small-framed doctor

---

[6] Personal Protective Equipment - injury or infection. (Personal Protective Equipment (PPE), n.d.)

from Bangladesh, he has worked at the hospital for twelve years and is well-liked by all the staff.

'Hello, Dr Patel. You are here early, considering you worked the night shift yesterday.'

He yawns. 'I haven't gone home.'

'You look exhausted!' Mum exclaims. Even under the protective equipment, she can see that he looks a little ashen. Then again, that could be from what he experienced on his recent shift, as much as being overworked.

Dr Patel waves his hand dismissively. 'I'm okay. For your information, two nurses just phoned in sick. The staff at the front desk will fill you in.'

Just then, Angelo walks in. 'Good morning, Gloria!' He chirps. Angelo is also a nurse. He is originally from the Philippines. 'I see you're still here, Dr Patel.'

Dr Patel nods wordlessly before walking off in the direction of the lift.

Mum can see the strain of working all night on Angelo's face. 'Morning Angelo, has your shift finished?'

'I have to stay on to help the other nurses,' he replies. 'They are all tired from rotating patients on their beds every two hours. It is affecting us all physically and mentally.'

A few colleagues have died from the virus. The rest are in a constant daze of tiredness. Just yesterday, Mum had an earpiece in her ear while working on the children's ward. She was listening to a colleague's funeral service.

'You can't give up now, dear.' She recalls saying to a young patient. 'Where there is life, there is hope.' The well-known words are all she can say to encourage her patients. But they are also true. No one can afford to lose hope during these dire times.

'June has been transferred to ICU[7],' Angelo adds. 'I know she is religious, so I played her some Bible readings on my small wireless speaker.' June and Jill, two sisters and both nursing staff at the hospital, caught the virus. Jill, the younger sister, died from organ failure last night.

'How distressing for their parents and the rest of the family,' Mum says wearily.

'Loretta washed, combed, and braided June's hair yesterday,' Angelo continues. 'She felt it was the least she could do for her colleague.' He walks behind the counter to locate a couple of files, slickly applying sanitiser from the red and white dispenser on the wall next to the cabinets. Everyone sanitises their hands at twenty-minute intervals. All day long.

He turns back to Mum. 'Gloria, do you recall when four members of one family were admitted that Monday morning? They were in separate wards. The ten-year-old daughter was in the ICU.'

---

[7] Intensive Care Unit

Mum takes her cue from Angelo and begins the routine of preparing for her ward rounds, starting with sanitising her hands, which she already did as she entered the building.

'Of course. Who could forget? I called the hospital chaplain to visit the girl in the end.' She fastens her visor adeptly. 'Sadly, she was so breathless that her condition deteriorated by Wednesday, and she died on Friday, despite receiving the maximum amount of oxygen.'

'Last night, once they concluded the inevitable would happen, the doctors gave permission for one member of Jill's family to visit the ward,' Angelo says. 'No-one came. Relatives are scared to come to the hospital even when they are allowed to.'

Mum lets out a loud breath. It is such a challenging period. 'It must have been a painful decision to make – avoid contact with the virus or risk spreading it at home.

'I have seen so many patients die alone in the hospital,' Angelo says, looking deeply saddened by the whole affair. 'It must be so tough.'

'I wouldn't like to be in Dr Patel's shoes either,' Mum reflects. 'He has to make difficult decisions on a case-by-case basis. Which patients should live, whose underlying health conditions could compromise recovery, and so on. It must be tough to manage multiple critically unwell patients every day.'

♦♦♦♦♦♦♦♦

It is time for the ward round. Mum is going around the beds with the senior medical team, nurses and junior doctors.

There are several people working in various roles as hospital staff, including those recalled from retirement and volunteers from the private sector. They hide behind masks and gowns, with many machines dispersed in between. Aside from doctors wearing stethoscopes, it is difficult sometimes to know who is doing what, as they rush from corridor to operating room to ward, attending to patients on ventilators with multiple tubes running in and out of their bodies.

Mum spots an empty bed and her stomach drops. It is one of two cases: the patient is off the ventilator and has been moved to the other end of the ward, which is good news, or the person has died. Mum and her colleagues hate this situation, but they face it every day. It will stay in their memories forever. The day is hectic, and she doesn't get a chance to ask what happened to the patient in the empty bed.

Time goes by in a blur, and it is soon six-thirty and time for Mum to start handing over. 'I like it when I am rushed off my feet like today,' She tells one of the nurses. 'Now, all I need is to hand over to Dawn and I can put it behind me until tomorrow.'

The nurse nods. 'Yes, it goes by so quickly, and we don't get time to think. About anything.' She leaves unsaid what everyone else is thinking. 'Oh, here she is!'

Dawn rushes up to Mum. 'Sorry I'm late, Gloria.' She is taking off her jacket and fumbling around with bits of her uniform. 'My daughter had another meltdown. She hates being cooped up indoors and not being able to see her friends.'

Mum greets her with a fatigued smile. 'You're only one hour late, Dawn. It's better than last time.' She pats her colleague on the shoulder. Dawn is having so much trouble with her family. The pandemic isn't just affecting lives in the hospital.

Mum has done more than a twelve-hour shift and is so tired. She hands over to Dawn before collecting her jacket and bag. As she walks toward the entrance, Mum spots Nigel, a retired veteran who has volunteered to be a hospital porter on the ground floor.

She waves at him. 'Bye, Nigel.'

'Mind how you go, Gloria.' He replies. People like Nigel are volunteering in different roles across the country. Human beings can be so kind and generous.

Dad is parked by the side entrance to the hospital. He hops out and comes round to open the door for Mum. 'You look shattered, love.'

She simply shakes her head as she takes the seat beside him. The drive home is quiet, and the streets are empty. She soon opens the door to the house.

'I'm home!' she shouts.

Adam and Dimple are seated on the couch watching television and they turn around to wave at her. She does not hug them. Instead, she strips off her uniform and other items of clothing by the porch, places them in the laundry basket and picks up her clean dressing gown from the coat hanger. Then, she goes straight to the bathroom for a very hot shower. Like the family members she and Angelo discussed earlier, she would not want to transmit any virus to Dimple, Adam, Nana or Dad.

When she comes out of the bathroom, Dimple is waiting by the door with a mug. 'How was work today, Mum?'

'We lost more patients, and unfortunately their families could not visit them before they died. That was the hardest part for me today.'

Dimple feels tears welling in her eyes, but she chokes them away. She has to be strong right now. Mum doesn't usually talk about her day in any detail, so it must have been especially difficult.

'That is so sad, Mum,' She says in a small voice. 'You look exhausted, you must be hungry.'

Mum shakes her head. 'Thanks darling. This cuppa is all I need right now.'

Too tired to eat, she goes straight to bed, but despite the fatigue, she is unable to sleep. She lies there, rehearsing the day's events. Could she or the doctors have done anything differently to avoid the forty-five deaths?

She closes her eyes but constantly hears machines beeping.

'We did everything possible.' She mutters drowsily before finally falling asleep.

She dreams about the day's experiences and can still feel the mask on her face.

*Dimple Dares to Ask*

# CHAPTER 10

## THE END OF YEAR 6 -
## 'WHY IS THERE NO SCHOOL TRIP?'

***July 2020***

The alarm clock on the table next to the single bed is ringing. It is 6am on a Friday morning, and there is an eerie green glow in the sky.

From under her lilac duvet bedcover, Dimple reaches out to stop the clock. Then she swiftly dives back under the sheets and closes her eyes again. A few minutes later, she jerks upright in the middle of a surreal dream.

*Mum is driving her towards the school gates, just as the school bus is leaving. Dimple waves frantically at the bus.*

*'Wait for me! Miss! Zainab! Natalie! Amara! You can't leave me behind,' she shouts. 'I'm coming on the school trip too. WAIT!'*

Just then, Mum knocks on her bedroom door. 'Dimple, you're going to be late for school if you don't get up now!'

Dimple rubs her eyes grouchily. 'There is no more school,' She mutters. 'What is school if I cannot play and chat with my friends? This lockdown is so unfair!'

Dimple recently found out where she will attend her first year in secondary school. She is apprehensive about starting 'big school', as Mum calls it.

For starters, even though Mum will drop her off in the morning, she will come back home on the school bus by herself. Also, none of her friends from Year 6 will be there. They are all going to different secondary schools apart from Zainab and Natalie, the lucky ones who might even be in the same class.

'It sucks!' Dimple says, grumpily leaving her bed to start getting ready.

For part of her final term, Dimple attends her primary school in person because her parents are essential workers who work for the NHS[8]. However, she must sit two metres away from her friends.

The children are placed in small classes of twelve, with extended breaks outdoors and shorter school days. They do not have a choice of who is in their bubble. When they are indoors, they have short breaks but cannot mix across groups. This is awkward for Dimple and her friends. Their teacher, Mrs Jones, also maintains her

---

[8] The National Health Service.

distance. She sits by the desk in front of the class and uses PowerPoint to teach the lesson.

At the end of the school day, Natalie picks up her school bag from the rack and heads towards the classroom door to go home.

Dimple spots her walking past the class and raises her hand. 'Miss, can I talk to Natalie, please?'

'Dimple, you know the rules,' Mrs Jones says. 'You are not allowed to mix with Natalie because she goes home at 3 and you finish at 5. You cannot interact outside your bubble.'

The following day, Mrs Jones sends an email to all her students:

*'The Year 6 End of Year play will not go ahead. This is because some students tested positive for Covid-19 and have to self-isolate at home. The leaver's disco is also cancelled.'*

The Year 6 students are upset. They have not been able to do a lot of stuff, won't see their schoolmates again, and will be leaving everyone behind.

Dimple shows the email to Mum and Dad. She has been rehearsing very hard for the school play. Teardrops run down her face.

Mum reaches into her bag for a tissue paper to wipe Dimple's face. 'Don't cry, Sweetie. I will call a Parent's Teachers Association meeting to see what we can do.'

Dimple retreats to her bedroom, still sobbing.

Mum calls up the other Year 6 mums on her phone list, including Zainab, Natalie, Favour, and Amara's mothers.

'We can't let the children down,' She tells them. 'Is there anything we can do so the play can go ahead?'

♦♦♦♦♦♦♦

Two days, several phone calls and Zoom meetings later, with the help of the teachers, school governors and a local theatre, they agree on a virtual solution where those isolating can interact and perform with their friends on stage.

Mum arrives home from work around 7pm. The living room is empty. Dimple, who would normally be watching her favourite television programme is nowhere to be found. Mum shakes her head and steps near the staircase.

'Dimple? I'm home!' She calls her daughter a second time. Still no reply, so she goes up to Dimple's bedroom.

She taps the door gently, calling Dimple's name a third time. 'Are you asleep?'

A voice mumbles from under the duvet. 'No, Mum. I'm just lying down.'

Mum pulls back the cover. Dimple is lying on her stomach. Mum taps her shoulder. 'Sweetie, I have good news! The show will still go on.'

Dimple looks at her hopefully. 'Really? But, how?'

'The isolating students will take part from home while others will perform on the school stage as planned.'

'Do you mean a virtual participation?'

'Yes, the PTA members will work with the school governors and a team from the Shaftesbury Theatre to work out the logistics.'

Dimple bounces up to give her Mum a big hug. 'Thanks Mum, you're the best!'

'I know how hard you've been rehearsing,' Mum replies. 'And I cannot miss seeing my daughter on her primary school stage one final time.'

♦♦♦♦♦♦♦

Dimple is going to miss going on the annual school trip at the end of the year. She has been looking forward to going away for a week with her friends on the trip, which, according to Mrs Jones, was organised by 'the leading outdoor education provider who delivers inspirational learning through adventure for young people, teachers, group leaders and parents'. Mrs Jones had said that several times throughout the year.

Instead, the Headteacher, Mr Singleton announces during assembly that the Education Minister has banned school trips because of the lockdown restrictions.

'I can't believe the school trip is cancelled!' Dimple whispers to Zainab and Natalie. The girls have sneakily managed to sit next to each other during the assembly, albeit two metres apart. 'I got Mum to order me a pink jacket just for the trip. Now I can't even show my jacket off to anyone!'

Zainab shushes her. 'You don't want to get into trouble with Mr Singleton.'

'I was looking forward to the trip, too,' Natalie mumbles somewhat loudly under her breath. 'I need some quiet time away from the two-year-olds!'

'No!' Dimple says, smiling at Natalie. 'Your twin sisters are sweet.'

Natalie rolls her eyes. 'Not if you live under the same roof with them. Rachel and Rochelle are always screaming and running around the house. Our neighbour calls them Double Trouble. She is right.'

'I was looking forward to the school trip too,' Zainab chips in' 'This was going to be my holiday for the year as Mum says we cannot afford to travel abroad this year.'

Natalie turns to look at her. 'Why is that?'

'Shh!' Zainab says again and then continues, 'Mum says everything has gone up in price this year. My new school blazer and the other school uniforms cost a fortune, apparently.'

'Since Mum had the twins, we have not gone on any overseas holidays,' Natalie adds, pulling at her hair. 'She has not gone back to work after having the twins, and she says it's a luxury to travel abroad now.'

Dimple hushes them both, then whispers, 'I guess it doesn't matter much now, anyway, since everything is being cancelled. I overheard Miss talking to Amara's mum about the end of year activities. Apparently, the End of Year award ceremony will be different too.'

♦♦♦♦♦♦♦♦

The children are on the school's big field for the graduation ceremony, with each class of twelve sitting two meters apart. A camera is set up to project a live broadcast.

Dimple has worked really hard on her schoolwork, but, in the end, everyone receives the same pack containing a general certificate and a frame with all the students' names on the shape of a cross from their Catholic school.

'I was hoping to win the Academic Person of the Year award,' Dimple says miserably.

'And I wanted to win the award for Best Art Student,' Zainab adds.

'I just hoped to beat Lucky in the mathematics category,' Natalie grumbles. 'Now we'll never know who is better in Mathematics.'

'I still think girls are smarter.' Dimple announces. 'You would have won the Mathematics prize, Natalie.'

*Dimple Dares to Ask*

# CHAPTER 11

## FOOD RATIONING - 'WHY ARE THE SHELVES EMPTY?'

***13 August 2020***

*Ping! Ping! Ping!*

Aunty Nadia sits up in bed, half-awake, not feeling like doing anything today. Her shift at the supermarket starts in less than an hour, and she has an important event as well. She started there as a Saturday casual worker and worked part-time throughout her University days.

She puts her right palm to her forehead and groans. Her head has been throbbing for the past two days.

*Ping!* Goes her phone again. She frowns, then realises it's the NHS Covid-19 app. She picks it up to read the text message.

*You need to self-isolate until 23 August at 23:59.*

'Heavens! The Regional Manager is coming to inspect the store today!' She exclaims. Then she closes the app and calls her deputy manager.

'Hi Jason. You won't believe what just happened.'

'You got pinged?' Jason says jokingly.

'Yep.'

'What? I was joking!' He sounds mortified.

'It's true. I have to self-isolate for 10 days.'

'Okay, Nadia. I'm sure it's nothing. I will leave for work now to be there before the Regional Manager arrives. Do you want me to inform the Human Resources department?'

'I'll do that after this call, thanks. All the best with the inspection today.'

'I can hear the disappointment in your voice,' Jason says sympathetically. 'You've been looking forward to it all month.'

They hang up, and Nadia dials Head Office.

'Dimple, get my phone from my bag and let Aunty Nadia know we are on our way to the supermarket,' Mum says, reversing her car into the main road. There aren't many people driving on the road at this hour and the street is calm.

Dimple dials her aunt's number.

Aunty Nadia picks up. 'Hi Gloria. I was just going to call…'

'It's Dimple, Aunty. Mum is driving.'

*Food Rationing - 'Why are the shelves empty?'*

'Is everything alright?'

'Yes, Aunty, Mum says to let you know we are on our way.'

'Oh, alright then. But I won't be at work today.'

'You sound strange, Aunty.' Dimple says. 'Are you alright?'

'I've just been pinged to self-isolate for 10 days. How are you and the rest of the family?'

'We're all fine,' Dimple replies. She covers the mouthpiece of the phone and passes the message over to Mum.

'Tell Nadia I'll call her when we get home.'

Dimple relays the message.

'Alright dear, I'll talk to you later.' Aunty Nadia disconnects the call.

Five minutes later, Dimple is pushing a trolley beside Mum. Mum is looking for the hand soap, but the shelf is empty. The supermarket is busier than usual, and everyone is wearing a face mask. Dimple's mask is pink. Across the shop floor, two-metre markings in blue ink remind customers of the social distancing rules:

*Please be careful not to invade other people's space.*

*Please stay at least two metres away from other customers.*

The arrows also provide a one-way route, so customers keep to their right side when moving around the shop floor.

'Gloria! Dimple!'

Dimple looks up to see Franklin, their next-door neighbour, pushing an almost empty trolley towards them. He stops a few metres from where they are standing, but he is clearly smiling under his mask. His eyes are gleaming.

They exchange pleasantries.

'It's nice to see you both. Conversations are sparse these days. By the way, where is Nana?'

'Nana is resting at home.' Dimple explains. 'She has a slight headache.'

Franklin steers his trolley sideways to avoid colliding with another shopper. 'I hope she feels better soon.'

'Thanks, Franklin. She should be fine after taking some pain relievers,' Mum says. 'My sister, Nadia, who manages this store was pinged by the Covid-19 NHS app this morning and is now self-isolating for ten days. We're hoping it's nothing to worry about.'

Franklin shakes his head slowly. 'Sorry to hear that. These are difficult times.'

As they talk on, Mum grabs two pineapples off the shelf. Dimple is excited because Mum plans to make her delicious tropical fruit salad.

'I can hardly find any item on my shopping list,' Franklin says.

Mum examines the pineapples closely. They are just beginning to ripen. 'I remember hearing something about food shortages,' She replies.

'That is because there has been little or no stock delivery since the beginning of last week. Lorry drivers are stuck in the European countries, particularly France!' Franklin sounds exasperated. 'I'll see you around, ladies. I'd better join the queue.'

They wave to him before continuing along the aisles.

The shelves are almost empty. Signs restrict each customer to one pack of toilet rolls, pasta, and three tins of chopped and plum tomatoes.

'Why is everyone in such a hurry, pushing past each other?' Dimple asks Mum.

'There is a shortage of food and essential items, Dimple. Because of the pandemic and Brexit, many lorry drivers are not bringing over our food supplies like they used to.'

'What is Brexit, Mum?'

A combination of "Britain" and "exit" Mum explains. 'It is the name given to the United Kingdom's departure from the European Union. Since we voted to leave, new laws must be made around how we trade.'

Dimple nods. 'So that's why most shelves are empty.'

They walk to the sixth aisle looking for their regular brand of tomato ketchup, but there are no sauces at all, not even the ones Dimple dislikes. Instead, a sign against the shelf reads:

*'Sorry, we're having some availability issues, which will be resolved shortly.'*

They move along. 'Don't forget my favourite ice cream, Mum,' Dimple pleads.

'Let's go and check for that,' Mum says, and they head for the end of the shop where the deep freezers are located.

Suddenly, Dimple lets go of the shopping trolley. Mum tightens her grip to prevent it rolling down the aisle. 'Whatever is the matter, Sweetie?'

SWOOSH…! Dimple bolts forward like a sprinter, dives into the ice cream cabinet and snatches the last tub of strawberry ice cream, brushing aside a middle-aged woman in a red coat with rollers in her hair. Her head is covered with a grey scarf.

'What…?' is all she can say before Dimple scarpers back to Mum with the tub in both hands.

'Wow! Where did 'Usain Bolt' emerge from?' Mum is laughing. 'I didn't know you had that fire in you, Dimple. I will tell the others when we get home.'

Dimple smirks and places her hard won ice cream in the trolley.

Mum apologises to the woman with rollers in her hair.

'Kids, eh?' The woman replies, shaking her head in bewilderment.

Dimple happily ignores the conversation. She is thinking of the fantastic dinner and dessert they will enjoy tonight. She hops alongside Mum to the checkout. The queue is still long but slightly better than when they arrived.

Mum shows her staff ID card to a member of staff.

'Follow me please,' the woman says, leading Mum to a priority till. Soon it is their turn at the checkout. Dimple helps Mum put the items on the conveyor belt, ticking off the list as she goes along:

*1 24-pack of toilet paper*

*1 hand sanitiser gel (none)*

*1 packet of painkillers*

*1 tub of strawberry ice cream*

*2 loaves of bread*

*4 pints of milk*

*1 pack of kitchen towels*

*Toothpaste (none)*

*1 500-gram bag of rice*

The checkout assistant's face mask matches the store's colours. 'And how are you today, young lady?' She asks Dimple.

'Very well, thanks,' Dimple says, lifting the strawberry ice cream onto the conveyor belt. She looks around for the woman with rollers in her hair, and sure enough, she is on the same level with them at the next till.

'Make sure you enjoy that LAST tub of strawberry ice cream!' she tells Dimple.

'She's not very happy with you, Dimple,' Mum says, still checking out her shopping list. 'I can hear it in her voice.

Dimple shrugs and starts looking at her phone.

The checkout assistant scans the last item and Mum looks at the till for the final amount. At the top of the till, a sign reads,

*'Due to the present situation with the pandemic, we advise our customers to pay by card where possible. This is the safest way to protect customers and staff from spreading the virus.'*

Mum pays with her bank card. 'Thank you and keep safe,' She says to the cashier.

# CHAPTER 12

## EXAM RESULTS - 'WHAT GRADES WILL ADAM GET?'

***August 2020***

'Adam gets his exam results today,' Dimple announces as she enters Nana's bedroom. The room has just been renovated. Now, Nana doesn't have to traipse upstairs to use the bathroom in the middle of the night.

A double bed is in the corner, and a large screen television is on a cabinet by the bed. The dressing table is situated by another door that leads to the kitchen. There is a single armchair at the bottom of the bed. Opposite Nana's bed is a table and chair, and her Bible is in a black leather case on the table. An open book with a pen in the middle lies next to the Bible. Nana was writing before Dimple came in.

'I have been praying for your brother.' Nana replies. 'I know he will get good grades. What time is he going to pick up his results?'

'I'm not sure, but I will go upstairs and ask him now.'

♦♦♦♦♦♦♦

Adam is lying face up on his bed. His eyes are wide open and have been since he went to bed at 9pm the night before. The sun is slowly coming in through the blinds.

His bedroom, first left at the top of the stairs, is decorated in green, his double bed to the left as you enter the room. Posters of classic cars are all around the room –a black Jaguar E-Type, a Porsche 924, a red BMW and a dark blue Chevrolet Corvette. Opposite his bed is a poster of The Time Bridge Squad.

His mind whirling, Adam turns to his left side, then to his right, and back to the left. Finally, he gets up and strolls across to his chair and desk in the corner where his silver laptop and schoolbooks sit as though waiting for his attention. A framed picture of a smiling Marcus, in a red jersey holding a football under his arm, rests to the left of the desk. For once, Marcus' smile doesn't fill Adam with pleasure.

Adam plans to collect his GCSE results from school today. He has worked hard since the year started, so he would generally be confident of getting good grades. But this year is different because the government cancelled all exam papers. All students will be graded on teacher assessments throughout the year.

'Will my teachers think I have done enough to pass my exams?' he wonders, stashing his laptop into his school bag. 'What if I don't pass my core subjects? What if I have to repeat the school year?' the thoughts continue running through his mind.

Dad had been home-schooling Adam during the holiday. The teachers sent the course materials online, and Adam would work through them with Dad. He and Adam still managed to have regular breaks, and on good days, with Dad working from home, they sometimes went for lunch hour football kick abouts in the park.

'If you get good grades, I will take you to watch the end of season game for the Time Bridge squad,' Dad had promised.

Adam was thrilled.

'You have to get the grades first,' Dad reminded him often.

'No worries, Dad. I will put all my effort into this year's exams.' But he did not even get a chance to do that. He must wait for a couple more hours before he gets his grades.

Months earlier, he had been delighted with Marcus' signed football shirt that Dimple brought back from Paphos. If things didn't go well, he would have to settle for that as his reward for the work.

He sighs and returns to his bed where he crawls under the covers, slips on his earphones and starts listening to some RnB music.

A knock on the door is followed by Dimple's voice entering the room. 'Phew! Your room stinks, Adam.' She marches across the room and opens a window. 'Why didn't you put your trainers out to air when you got back yesterday? Jeez!'

Adam tries to see his room through her eyes. His clothes are strewn all over the floor – dirty socks, face towel, boxers. But he doesn't care about any of that. Exam results are looming.

Dimple isn't finished with her nagging. 'Yuck! What type of crust is this under your table? Pizza or a piece of left-over toast?'

She pulls the sheet away from him and sits on the side of his bed. 'Nana wants to know when you're going to collect your results.' Then her tone softens. 'How do you feel, Adam?'

'I honestly don't know. A little anxious, I guess,' he grumbles. 'I keep wishing I had sat for my exams like the previous year 11s.'

'You don't have to be scared,' Dimple assures him. 'There's not much you can do at this stage, anyway, since your papers have been marked, but I'm sure you'll be fine. You did your best, too. Don't fear the worst.'

She pats him on the shoulder and leaves the room.

Adam pulls himself out of bed, has a quick shower and puts on his lucky polo shirt, jeans and a black baseball cap. He grabs his black leather jacket at the front door and hurries off to school before the rest of the family start gathering in the kitchen.

As he approaches the school gates, he has a feeling of nostalgia. He spent five memorable years in this building.

'I can't believe I'm done with secondary school,' He mutters to himself, remembering his first day in Year 7. 'It seems like yesterday when I met Ollie in the school corridor.'

Adam was looking around shyly for the English class, and, according to Ollie, he looked lost in the school corridor. Ollie approached him and they both found their way to the class. They became inseparable. Jay joined them in Year 9, and the three formed a close bond.

He spots his friends and waves. 'Jay! Ollie!'

The boys traipse up to him and they stand awkwardly in an unspoken but shared sentiment. Exam results day in 2020. The Great Unknown.

'How have you been?' Ollie asks Adam.

'Not bad, thanks. Sad that I could not go on holiday with Mum and Dimple.'

They enter the school hall which is not busy as students are not allowed to stay inside after collecting their results. They look for their teacher and collect the brown envelopes containing their results.

Adam tears up the envelope and hurriedly scans through the details.

'Seven As and Five Bs!' He exclaims. 'The Biology assessment was really hard. I didn't expect a B.' He smiles for the first time today. 'I hope Dad will still take me to the end of season Time Bridge game, although I don't think he will be happy with five Bs!'

Ollie gives Adam a man-hug. 'Well done, Bruv!'

'Have you opened your envelope?' Adam asks him.

Ollie shakes his head. He takes a deep breath and peels the envelope open. '1 A*, 6 As, 5 Bs!' Ollie reports, staring at his certificate. 'Mum won't believe it. She kept saying I was not studying hard enough. She is hard to please, but I'm glad I've proved her wrong.'

Jay gives each boy a fist pump. 'Well done, man!'

'What about your result, Jay?' Adam and Ollie ask at the same time.

'7 As and 5 Bs as well. Mum will be so happy; she'll be on the phone to her friends tonight. Her first son has passed his GCSE exams!' His relief is evident in his big smile. Another hush falls over the trio as each recalls his own experience of the past six months.

Adam breaks the silence. 'I don't feel like going home yet. I'm still trying to figure out what Dad's reaction will be.'

'Let's go to McDonald's,' Ollie suggests. 'We can celebrate even if our parents won't. It's been a hard year and we've had a lot to cope with.'

'Sure, why not?' Jay says. 'Zoom and Teams classrooms were tough for any sixteen-year-old to handle.'

The other two nod companionably, then they all set off for the nearest McDonald's. After eating, they make their way to the local park to play a game of football.

Just then, Adam's phone rings. It's Mum.

'Where are you, Adam?'

'On my way to the park. I'm going to play football with Ollie and Jay.'

'What about your exam results?'

'Oh, it's alright.' Adam says. 'I was just about to call and let you know I had 7 As and 5 Bs.'

'That's great! Well done, Son.' She sounds genuinely pleased. 'Why don't you come home before going out with your friends?'

'No, Mum. See you later. Love you!' He hangs up and runs to catch up with his friends.

When they get to the park, they put their rucksacks together under a tree and cover the bags with their jackets. One or two people walking their dogs and a few runners are in the park, but it is very big and there is enough distancing room for everyone.

Six boys of the same age group are doing a throw around with a ball. Adam and his friends join them, and a football game starts.

*Dimple Dares to Ask*

# CHAPTER 13

## HAPPY BIRTHDAY, DIMPLE – 'WHY IS MUM SHOUTING MY NAME?'

*September 2020*

It is Saturday 6 September. Dimple is lying on her bed, staring at her wall clock, which has been ticking loudly since she opened her eyes. She is twelve years old today. She has been awake and fidgety since five o'clock, trying hard to stay quiet to avoid waking everyone else up.

She exhales loudly. 'Why is it only 7 o'clock?'

She sighs again.

*'Why are they still asleep?'* She wonders irritably. *'Don't they know how important today is?'*

She gets up, stands in front of her wardrobe mirror and runs her fingers through her plaits. Jade, Mum's favourite hair stylist, came to the house after school yesterday, and Dimple's curly hair has been beautifully braided to shoulder length, although she had to sit still for five hours and forty minutes to get it done. Jade cleverly added blue beads to the ends of the plaits to make them even prettier.

Dimple peeks left and right outside her bedroom door, but there is no one in sight. The house is so silent, you can hear a pin drop. She returns to her bed and closes her eyes, but she is restless.

'Wake up, Dimple!' Mum suddenly calls across the landing.

Dimple stretches lazily. *Finally*! *But why is Mum shouting my name? She must know I have been awake for ages!*

'Dimple? Are you awake?' Mum calls again. 'Dad has something for you!' She sounds happy. Everyone in the family is always happy on birthdays.

'Coming!' Dimple shouts, shooting to her feet and rushing out of her room. She skids as she runs into Mum and Dad's bedroom, where her father is sitting on the edge of the bed. Mum has gone downstairs.

'Happy Birthday, Baby,' Dad says, smiling.

'Thank you, Daddy.' Dimple replies, stretching out her hand. 'Birthday present, please?'

Dad gets up and goes over to Mum's dressing table. He picks something up, which he hides behind him.

'Guess what I have here?'

Dimple groans. 'Daaad!' Her father likes to joke around, but she is not in the mood today. 'Let me see, let me see, please!'

Dad promised her a good present because she worked super hard during the lockdown terms. Mrs Jones had also reported that Dimple was one of the most well-behaved pupils on Teams and in person. Dimple cannot wait to see her reward.

Dad walks over to her. 'Okay, okay, Scamp! Close your eyes and turn around.'

'What is it?' Dimple asks, even as she obediently shuts her eyes and turns her back to him.

'Patience,' Dad says. His voice is near her ear. Then she feels him placing something around her neck. Next, Dad holds both her shoulders and guides her across the room.

'You can open your eyes now.'

Dimple opens her eyes. She is standing before Mum's dressing table mirror. Around her neck is a gold-plated necklace! It has a little lilac cubic pendant that reads *Dimple* in gold lettering.

'Oh, Daddy!' Dimple breathes. 'It's so beautiful.'

Dad envelops her in a giant, squishy hug. Her dad gives the best hugs, Dimple thinks.

'Happy Birthday, Sweetie. I know we had plans to travel for your 12th birthday, but we can't do that anymore because of the pandemic.' She can hear the regret in his voice.

'That's okay, Daddy.' Dimple replies cheerfully. Her parents have organised a birthday party at their local park, and she couldn't be any more excited. She starts chattering as she and Dad walk downstairs for breakfast.

'My best friends from Year 6 are coming! I can't wait to see Zainab, Natalie, Amara, Charlie, Favour, and David.' She skips down the staircase. 'I haven't seen them since we left school. I know…, I have seen some of them on FaceTime and Zoom, but it's not the same.

'Careful, Dimple!' Dad interjects. 'You don't want to spend your birthday at the Accident and Emergency department, now, do you?'

'Dad! The hospitals are too busy dealing with COVID patients. I'm not silly enough to get injured!' But she slows down. She really does not want to end up in hospital. Her friend Charlie's aunt went into hospital to see the doctor and got infected with the virus. Thankfully, it was mild, and she could go home after being in hospital for five days.

After a hurried breakfast with the family, Dimple goes to her room and puts on a light pink top over her favourite pair of blue jeans and slightly heeled shoes.

Mum pops her head around the door. 'You look lovely, Poppet.' She looks tearful.

'Are you crying, Mum?' Dimple is tying her shoe straps, but she stands up and hurries towards her mother.

Mum hugs Dimple. 'No, darling. I'm just thinking of what a difficult year it has been and being grateful that we get to celebrate your birthday.' She wipes her face with the back of her hand and smiles brightly. 'Now, what else are you wearing today?'

Dimple looks at her bed and reaches a decision. 'I think I will wear the purple birthday hat. She picks up the hat and pulls the white string over her chin. 'I'm ready!'

Just then, Nana comes in with a big, pink and black tote bag around her left shoulder. Something seems to be moving inside it.

'What's in the bag, Nana?' Dimple asks.

But her grandmother isn't giving anything away. 'Guess.'

'I can't! I'm sure I'll get it wrong.'

Nana hands the bag over. It feels warm. Dimple unzips it and peeks inside. She looks up. Adam and Dad are also in her room. 'Awesome!' She squeals. 'It's a poodle in a poodle tote bag! Look at the lovely pink ribbons over her ears. Thank you very much, Nana. You're the best Nana in the whole wide world!'

Nana kisses her on the forehead. 'You're most welcome, darling.'

Dimple circles her arms around Nana and plants a long kiss on her cheeks. Then she turns to her mother.

'Mum…? Did you know about my poodle?'

'No, darling.' But Mum's smile says she knew all about it. 'What will you call her?'

'Kitty.' Dimple replies immediately. 'Her name is Kitty.'

♦♦♦♦♦♦♦

As noon beckons, the sun is coming out, and the weather is dry. Mum has organised for two tents to be set up in the centre of the park. One for the deejay's equipment and the other for the food and drinks.

The tents are decorated with lilac (can you tell that this is Dimple's favourite colour?) and white balloons.

Aunty Nadia, Mum's sister, has ordered Dimple's favourite cupcakes from *N'ESSENCE Cakes*. The lilac sponge cupcakes are hanging from a silver tray, some topped with Oreo chocolate and others with wafer biscuits.

'You look lovely,' Aunt Nadia says to Dimple. 'At times like this, I miss not having a girl of my own.'

Dimple gives her aunt a peck on the cheek. 'I'm your daughter, too, remember?'

A giant white and lilac cylindrical birthday cake sits on the centre table. The number 12 is engraved with musical notes on its sides and HAPPY BIRTHDAY DIMPLE in lilac icing at the base. On top of the cake, twelve different coloured candles encircle a silver microphone. Dimple loves to sing, just like Nana.

'Happy Birthday, Dimple!' A voice calls out from a few yards away. It is Amara, who recently joined her class and who is in the same bubble with her.

Dimple runs up to her, and the two girls jump around, squealing excitedly.

'Here's your present,' Amara says, handing over a gift in foil silver wrapping paper. She greets Dimple's mum and dad before sitting on one of the chairs in front of the food tent.

Other friends gradually arrive, along with David, Samuel and Michael, Dimple's cousins, and Dimple is soon surrounded by a pile of presents.

The boys go off to play football while the girls chat happily in front of the food tent. The deejay starts playing some music, and Dimple's friends immediately request the song '*Love Yourself*' by Justin Bieber. The girls start dancing while the boys continue with their football game.

After a while, Mum serves the food with Aunty Nadia's help. Everyone is having a good time. Adam arrives with two of his friends, says hello to his cousins, grabs some food from Mum, which he eats quickly with his friends before disappearing again.

Dimple opens her gifts one by one. Suddenly, they hear a loud roar coming from the other end of the park. Dimple and her friends look up.

'It's a b-b-bear!' Her friend Favour says shakily.

The girls laugh. Favour gets scared at the slightest thing.

'It's someone dressed up as a bear, you silly goose.' Zainab retorts, still laughing.

Magic Man, the party entertainer Dad hired, reaches them and gives another hefty growl. 'Where is the birthday girl?' He is waving his big brown paws.

'It's me!' Dimple squeaks, raising her left hand.

Magic Man gives her an elbow bump. 'A gold crown and gold wand for the princess!' he announces solemnly, replacing her purple birthday hat.

Dimple feels like a Princess, so she feigns a courtesy bow to everyone.

Her friends clap excitedly.

The 'bear' leads them in party games, including pass the parcel, musical chairs, and Give *Us a Clue*.

# CHAPTER 14

## LITTLE CHEF DIMPLE - 'WHAT IS IN THE OVEN?'

*October 2020*

'What can we do to help the NHS, Mum?' Dimple asks one morning.

'We're doing our bit already,' Mum replies. 'We do the shopping for Mable, who lives alone two doors away.'

'But we can do more.' Dimple insists. 'Can we bake cakes for the staff at your hospital?'

Mum is impressed. 'That's an excellent idea, Dimple, even if it's because you like licking the spoon after mixing the ingredients!'

Dimple giggles. 'That's true.'

So, today, Dimple is in the kitchen with Mum, making cupcakes to be delivered to the hospital's receptionists, nurses, doctors, cleaners and all the other staff.

Dimple puts out the mixing bowl and ingredients, which include eggs, flour, mashed bananas, chocolate chips, slivered almonds, various spices, diced fruits and several other items. Mum creams some butter and sugar together. Dimple beats the eggs in, a little at a time, while Mum folds in the flour with a large metal spoon, adding a little milk until the mixture is ready. Next, Mum preheats the oven and Dimple lines five twelve-cup muffin trays with paper cases. They are going to make 60 cupcakes. Mum puts the tins in the oven to bake for 10-15 minutes, and the cupcakes turn golden-brown.

Dimple puts on her green jumper with her matching pair of jeans. Kitty is dressed in a green coat to match. Mum drives to the hospital, and Dimple sits in the back with Kitty on her lap.

The journey does not take long. Mum parks in the Accident and Emergency car park and walks towards the main entrance with Dimple and Kitty in tow. She squeezes out some sanitiser gel by the doors and rubs her hands thoroughly. Dimple hands Kitty and the basket to Mum and does the same.

The receptionist greets them as they enter the hospital through the wide sliding doors. There is a patient talking to a second receptionist in the other cubicle.

'Hello Dimple! What brings you here today?'

'I brought you some cupcakes, Tracey. I made them today with Mum.'

Tracey breaks out into a smile. 'Oh, you wonderful girl! How very sweet of you.'

'You can have as many as you want,' Dimple says, feeling pleased. They made more than enough for everyone.

'What is the atmosphere like today?' Mum asks quietly.

Tracey glances at Dimple, who is across the room studying a poster. 'We are very stretched.' She speaks in an undertone, too.

'You look tired. I miss the ever-positive vibrant Tracey with the happy smile.'

'I struggle to see the positive side at the moment, Gloria. One day rolls into another and it is just a grim picture.'

Mum nods and gives her a pat on the shoulder. 'I know. Please make sure everyone on duty gets some cake. I'll see you tomorrow on the morning shift.

'Thanks, Gloria.' Tracey speaks in a louder voice as Dimple makes her way back to the reception desk. 'I'll make sure to tell everyone the cakes are from Dimple.' She winks at Dimple. 'Young lady, I will enter you in the next series of *Junior Bake-off.*'

Dimple beams happily. 'Thanks, Tracey, stay safe!'

It's 8:45pm that evening. Mum walks in to see Dimple in the living room reading *Tomorrow Will Be A Good Day* by Captain Tom.

Dimple sets the book down. 'I'll bet you don't know who Captain Tom is, Mum?'

'I sure do,' Mum replies. 'He's the war veteran who raised nearly £33 million for the NHS walking 100 laps around his garden before his hundredth birthday. Am I right?'

'Yes, and he recorded a charity cover single of *You'll Never Walk Alone,* becoming the oldest person to get a UK number one,' Dimple adds.

Mum looks at her curiously. 'How do you know all this about Captain Tom?'

Dimple points at *Tomorrow Will Be A Good Day.* 'Natalie gave me his book as a belated birthday present.'

'That sounds interesting, Can I read it after you?'

'Sure, Mum, for a small fee.'

'Cheeky! I'll remember that when you ask for some pocket money!' Mum fires back.

'Oh no. Just kidding, Mum!' Dimple backs off quickly. 'Of course, you can read the book when I finish. How inspiring to do all this big stuff at 100 years old! We must all do our best to help. Every little act of kindness goes a long way.

Later that night, the Prime Minister is talking on the 10 o'clock news:

*"... I want to thank the millions of people who have been putting up with these restrictions in their areas for so long. I want to thank local leaders who have stepped up, and local communities.*

*"...As you can see, ...your work has been paying off...but as we've also seen, ... in this country, alas as across much of Europe, the virus is spreading even faster than the reasonable worst-case scenario of our scientific advisers.*

*"From Thursday until the start of December, you must stay at home. You may only leave home for specific reasons, including: [he sets out the list as usual[9]... we will not ask people to shield in the same way again. However, we are asking those who are clinically extremely vulnerable to minimise their contact with others, and not to go to work if they are unable to work from home... Christmas is going to be different this year, very different, but it is my sincere hope and belief that by taking tough action now, we can allow families across the country to be together...*

*"Our friends in Belgium, France and Germany have had to take very similar action...We will get through this - but we must act now to contain this autumn surge. We are not going back to the full-scale lockdown of March and April...but from Thursday, the basic message is the same:*

*Stay at home. Protect the NHS. And save lives[10]."*

---

[9] Author's note in parenthesis.
[10] Source (Sky news – October 2020)

*Dimple Dares to Ask*

# CHAPTER 15

## FAMILY CHRISTMAS – 'WHERE IS THE TURKEY?'

*December 2020*

Dimple thunders down the stairs to the ground floor. She is yelling at the top of her voice. 'Where is everyone? The meeting with Aunty Nadia is in 10 minutes! Nana, are you ready?'

'Yes, love. I'm just putting my slippers on.' Nana is dressed in a cream turtleneck top, a navy-blue skirt, and very thick, black tights. 'I need my comfy slippers, or my feet will get cold.'

'It's not that cold today, Nana!' Dimple says absentmindedly, darting around the house. 'Mum! Dad! Where are you?'

'In here, love,' Mum answers from the pantry. 'I'm getting some nibbles and drinks ready for our Zoom meeting.'

'What can I do to help?'

'You can get the little serving plates and kitchen towels.'

'No problem!' Dimple rushes to the kitchen.

Nana enters the pantry, which is adjacent to her bedroom. 'Hello Gloria, what are you preparing?'

'A few pies, some potato crisps, and cakes. The Zoom meeting will probably take ages, so we need supplies.' Mum exits the pantry balancing two trays stacked with assorted snacks, cans of soft drinks, bottles of water and two *Shloer* bottles against her chest.

Just then, Adam saunters in with Dad on his tail. They hurry over to help Mum with the trays.

Dad sets the tray he is carrying on the dining table. 'What's the meeting with Nadia about, again?'

'The family Christmas dinner,' Mum says. 'To discuss who is bringing what this year.'

Adam chuckles. 'Remember last year? Mum and Aunty kept arguing about who forgot the Christmas crackers.'

'Nadia was meant to get them from her store,' Mum insists. 'Somehow, she thought I was going to order them online.'

Adam shoots back up the stairs and returns a few moments later. 'I'll connect my laptop to the telly, so we can all use the same screen.'

'That is probably best,' Dad says. They enter the living room and Adam casts from his laptop to the large-screen wall-mounted television.

'I'm sitting on the lone sofa!' Dad says cheekily to Nana.

Nana taps him on the shoulder. 'You must be joking.' He moves over to sit with Mum, and Nana settles into her favourite chair.

Adam flicks the remote control, and several faces appear on the screen. There is Nana, Dad, Mum, Adam, Dimple, Aunty Nadia, Samuel and Michael. 'Hi Samuel. Hi everyone,' Adam says.

'Hello!' Samuel is waving.

'What are you up to these days?' Dad asks Samuel.

'I'm in sixth form now, Uncle,' He replies.

'You seem to have grown since we last saw you,' Dad responds. 'How tall are you now, and what subjects are you taking?'

'Six feet. Mum says I shot up like a bamboo tree after eating all the food at home during lockdown. As to your second question, I am taking Maths, Economics and IT.'

Aunt Nadia bumps into the conversation. 'Hi everyone.'

'Are we all here?' Mum asks.

'David will be joining us later, but we can start now,' Aunty Nadia replies.

'Who will say a short prayer before we start the meeting?' Mum wants to know.

'I'll pray,' Dimple says. *'Dear Jesus, thank you for the gift of family. Thank you for protecting us from this Coronavirus. Help us as we plan our Christmas dinner, and please provide for those who cannot afford a Christmas dinner with family like ours, Amen.'*

'Amen,' Everyone echoes. It takes a few seconds as their voices bounce across Zoom with the usual delays.

'What are you having for tea, Gloria?' Aunty Nadia asks.

'I made some prawn cocktail canapes with toast,' Mum replies.

'We're having grilled gizzard with plantain,' Aunty Nadia says.

Nana puts in a request. 'I hope you'll bring grilled gizzard with plantain when you come over for Christmas, Nadia.' Everyone loves Aunty Nadia's specialty.

'Of course.' Aunty Nadia says matter-of-factly. 'So, what else are we having for Christmas this year?'

Adam speaks up. 'I don't want turkey. Could we please have something else?

'You know your Dad will not accept that,' Nana points out.

Dad is nodding. 'That's right. We only have turkey once a year. At Christmas.'

Michael joins in the conversation. 'But we are fed up with turkey. We've been having it since I was born!'

'Well, nothing stops us from having a choice this time,' Nana suggests. 'What do people want to see on the Christmas table?'

'Duck,' Aunty Nadia proposes.

'Chicken!' Dimple and Michael say in unison.

Dad refuses to be left out. 'Turkey, and the biggest one in store!'

'That is greedy, Dad,' Dimple says.

'I call it well-deserved after a year of challenges and suffering,' Dad says roundly. The adults on the Zoom call can be heard agreeing with him, Aunty Nadia included. 'Who is making a note of these requests?'

'I will,' Samuel says. 'Can I hear everyone's preferences again, please?'

'What day of the week is Christmas day this year?' Nana asks.

Adam checks the calendar on his phone. 'It's on a Friday, Nana.'

'How many people are we expecting this year?' Dad asks.

'Just the two families,' Mum replies.

'… plus, Mable,' Nana adds.

'Have you invited her?' Dad asks.

'Not yet, but she has no one to visit her,' Nana says. 'I think she would be very pleased to join us.'

Dimple adds up the numbers. 'That's nine family members, plus Aunt Mable. Ten people in total.'

Michael puts his hand up on screen. 'Who is doing the quiz this year?'

'I can present the history quiz on Commonwealth countries that I used for my assignment,' Dimple offers.

David's face pops up on screen. 'That's hardly Christmas stuff.'

'Well, I got an 'A' for my work,' Dimple says proudly.

Everyone congratulates her on her hard work. 'Since it's going to be a long day, we could have more than one set of quizzes,' Nana suggests.

Dimple begins to giggle. 'Who can guess what Nana's Christmas day highlight will be?'

'The Queen's Speech!' everyone says together, bursting into peals of laughter.

Nana smiles at them fondly, grateful that they are all around to share this moment. 'Oh yes. I'm especially looking forward to Her Majesty's speech this year.'

'Who's bought all their presents already?' Adam asks.

'I've got all of mine, and all wrapped up too!' Nana says.

'Wow! Go Nana! Go Nana!' Dimple singsongs with a little jiggle.

'I ordered them online because the shops were not open when I wanted to do my shopping.'

'I might give out vouchers this year,' Aunty Nadia says. 'I'm being cautious about going out and about, looking for presents.'

The meeting goes on for another hour as everyone comes up with food, drink and game suggestions. With a mixture of seriousness and banter, they also recall their stories, concerns and experiences from the past year.

# CHAPTER 16

## NANA GETS HER VACCINE
## – 'DOES YOUR ARM HURT, NANA?'

*February 2021*

Dad is driving around the Time Bridge football stadium looking for a slot to park his car. Shared with the supermarket next door, the car park is busy. Adam usually plays football here every Sunday morning, but they are at the football grounds for a different reason today. It is February 2021 and Dad has brought Nana to have her vaccine, and Adam comes along too. The Covid-19 vaccination clinic is a make-shift tent beside the main football stadium.

They arrive at 3:15 pm but Nana's appointment is at 3:30. Since her invitation letter says not to arrive earlier than five minutes before the allotted time, Nana waits in the car with Dad and Adam.

'I am slightly disappointed,' she says. 'I thought the clinic would be in the main stadium.'

'Same here, Nana.' Adam replies from the back seat where he is playing on his iPad. 'Why did they mention the football stadium in your letter?'

'I suppose it makes the clinic easy to locate, since the stadium is popular around here.' Dad speculates, opening the glove compartment and handing everyone a face mask. At 3:25 pm, they wear their masks and enter through the white doors. Walking up to the sanitiser stand, they press the nuzzle in turns, rubbing the gel on their hands.

A volunteer staff shows Nana where to sit. 'I'm afraid your family will have to wait outside,' He tells her.

Dad and Adam return to the car.

The volunteer hands Nana another face mask which has been sanitised, and she discards the one Dad gave her in the car. She takes her seat, taking in the activities around her. It is not busy, and the stewards are moving people quickly through the queue. Soon enough, it is her turn.

'Please confirm your name, age, and address.' The receptionist says. She has an East European accent and is wearing a transparent covering over her face and mask.

'Mrs Patricia Robinson, 62, No 25 The Coppins, South West 11.'

'And how will you get back home after your vaccination, Mrs Robinson?'

'My son will drive me home,' Nana replies. 'We live a short distance from here. They are waiting for me in the car outside.'

The receptionist offers Nana a leaflet explaining the procedure. 'It also contains some frequently asked questions and answers,' She says pleasantly.

Nana thanks her and puts the leaflet in her handbag.

Some moments later, the receptionist sprays the tables and surrounding areas from a sanitiser bottle. A nurse in a blue and white uniform walks in.

'Mrs Robinson?'

'Yes!' Nana stands up.

'My name is Alyson, and I am your nurse today.'

'Nice to meet you,' Nana says before following her to the office.

'Do you have any questions?' Nurse Alyson asks. She has a friendly face which Nana can see through her eyes. Her mask obscures the rest of her face.

'Roughly how many people do you vaccinate in a day?'

'About four hundred people every day.'

'That's an encouraging figure.'

'We're just hopeful that we will meet the government's vaccination schedule target,' Nurse Alyson says, getting her injection and the rest of the kit out of her desk drawer. 'Do you have any concerns about the vaccine?'

'I have been reading about it, and still have some doubts. But my daughter-in-law is a nurse, and she has convinced me to take it. According to her, you have more resistance even if you catch the virus after taking the jab.'

Nurse Alyson nods. 'Which arm would you like me to inject?'

'The left, please,' Nana replies, rolling up her sleeve. 'I still have a scar on my right arm from my smallpox vaccination as a child.'

'I assure you; this vaccine will not leave a mark.'

Nana settles in her chair. 'That's good to know.'

'How many grandchildren do you have, Mrs Robinson?' Nurse Alyson continues, attempting to distract Nana. At the same time, she puts on a pair of disposable gloves and checks the information on the vaccine bottle. She shakes the bottle and draws out the clear liquid into the tiny injection. She then sterilises Nana's upper left arm with a wipe before inserting the needle.

'Well…,' Nana starts.

'There you are, Mrs Robinson!' the nurse says briskly. 'All done for you. You should have no pain, but if you do experience any, take two paracetamol tablets, and you will be fine.'

She wipes an alcohol swab over the area and covers it with a clear, white plaster. She clears away the needle pack, wipes down the desk with a sanitiser and discards the other items in a little bin by her desk. 'Please sit in

*Nana gets her vaccine – 'Does your arm hurt, Nana?'*

the waiting area for fifteen minutes before you leave. Have a good day, Mrs Robinson.'

'Thank you, Nurse Alyson.' Nana walks back to the waiting area, bewildered. Surely something should happen to her. But nothing happens.

Fifteen minutes later, she rings Dad, and they are on their way home. The streets are busy with people going about their normal duties as usual. Some are doing their shopping, and others are going for their evening stroll.

'How was it, Nana?' Adam asks.

'It was painless and quick, and I hardly felt a thing. I don't feel like I even got the vaccine.'

'Nana is as strong as an ox,' Dad says proudly.

'The nurse was gentle and friendly, which helped too,' Nana says. 'Everyone was out of the clinic within thirty minutes, including the fifteen minutes resting time before you are allowed to go home.'

'I'm pleased with the roll out of the vaccinations,' Dad says. 'We must give credit to the Government when it's due.'

Adam calls Dimple to tell her that they are nearly home. A little while later, Dimple opens the front door to let Nana, Adam, and Dad in.

In the living room, Nana sits on the single couch, Dimple slouches on a bean bag opposite her and Dad settles down to watch the television.

Adam makes his way up to his bedroom.

'Adam, don't forget to wash your hands.' Dimple reminds him.

'Yeah, Yeah!' Adam says. 'As if I could forget with you bugging me all the time.'

Dimple turns her attention to her grandmother. 'Does your arm hurt, Nana?'

Nana winces. 'It's just a little sore where the needle was inserted.'

'Does that mean you can no longer catch the virus?'

'I have to take the second vaccination to be completely protected,' Nana says thoughtfully. 'But even those who have been fully vaccinated can still catch, transmit and fall ill from the virus.'

'But my friends at school say that people who take the vaccinations are developing blood clots and getting sicker.'

Nana studies Dimple's face and sees a minor concern. Dimple is worried about her. She leans forward to pull her granddaughter into a comforting hug. 'Sweetheart, we are Christian soldiers. We are tough!'

She gives Dimple a quick squeeze, releases her and settles back into her seat. 'I am not afraid of the virus.' She continues. 'In Luke 10:19, we are told, "Behold, I give unto you power to tread on serpents and scorpions, and over all the power of the enemy: and nothing shall by any means hurt you." We cannot be harmed because we are well protected, Dimple.'

'Amen, Nana!' Nana always has a Bible verse for every situation, and Dimple finds it very reassuring today. But then, something else occurs to Dimple, and she places a hand on Nana's knee. 'Will there be enough vaccines for everyone in the country?'

'The Health Minister is working round the clock with other government officials to get enough supplies for everyone,' Dad interjects.

'And what happens if there are left-over vaccines, Dad?'

'The Government will decide what to do with them,' Dad replies. 'It will take a long time for the virus to go away, unfortunately, and it may be difficult for a while.'

Nana takes Dimple's face in her hands and gives her a great big smile. 'We must continue to have hope, not take avoidable risks, live healthily and take the necessary precautions.'

'Did you get a badge for your bravery today?' Dimple asks cheekily.

'You bet I did, young lady!'

'She is a strong lady indeed,' Dad adds. 'We Robinsons are made of the hard stuff!'

Dimple smiles and rolls her eyes at Dad. He says that all the time.

Mum pops her head out of the kitchen door. 'Would you like a cup of tea, Nana?'

'Yes, please, Gloria. But first, I must change out of these clothes.' She gets up and heads for her room.

Twenty minutes later, Nana returns to the living room and sits back down. Mum has set her tea in front of the couch where she was sitting. Nana bends down to pick it up but her phone rings.

'Hello, John.' She says into the receiver.

John sounds pleased to hear her voice. 'Hi Pat, I am phoning to find out how your vaccination went.'

'It was a seamless experience, John. Very quick with no pain at all. Have you booked your appointment yet?'

'I wasn't going to, but I booked it this morning. Sally was admitted to hospital yesterday and that got me thinking.'

'Poor Sally,' Nana says. 'She didn't look very well at all at the club on Wednesday.'

'She tested positive for Covid,' John continues. 'I suspect she also has an underlying condition.'

They talk briefly about other friends from the club.

'Take care of yourself, Patricia,' John says as they begin to round up. There is a slight note of concern in his voice.

'That's very kind of you, John. I definitely will.' Nana reassures him. 'You take care, too. Make sure you attend your appointment.'

They say their goodbyes and hang up.

# CHAPTER 17

## HANDS-FACE-SPACE - 'HOW WILL I REMEMBER THE RULES?'

*March 2021*

Adam is talking to Jay on the phone. 'Have you spoken to Ollie?'

'He's already on his way. Meet us by the bus stop.'

Adam is going to the supermarket where Aunty Nadia works. He and his friends have volunteered to help out at the vaccination centre stationed in the car park. He grabs his backpack and saunters into the kitchen to collect the packed lunch Mum has prepared for him.

'Thanks for the sandwiches, Mum!' He announces on his way out. 'See you both later!'

His parents turn to wave at him, but the door has already closed behind him.

'I am proud that Adam is using his summer break to help with the vaccination programme.' Dad tells Mum.

They are playing a game of chess to unwind after Mum's night shift.

'Me, too,' Mum says. 'One positive thing about this period is the young people demonstrating maturity and acting responsibly.'

♦♦♦♦♦♦♦

Adam and his friends arrive at the centre just before their shift starts. Adam stands by the entrance, handing out sanitized face masks as people come in. Ollie is sitting at the first desk of the bank of tables to the left of the tent. He is talking to a young lady who looks a little apprehensive.

'How are you feeling today, Miss...?'

'Sophie Mackintosh.'

'Hi, Sophie. My name is Ollie,' He says gently. 'Is this your first visit to the centre?'

She nods.

'I just need to confirm the information we have for you. Please state your age, address and postcode, and the name and address of your doctor.'

Sophie clears her throat. 'I am thirty-one years old.' She reels off her address and GP's details.

Ollie ticks the information on his folder. 'Thank you very much, Sophie.' He hands her a leaflet.

'"Hands. Face. Space[11]." She reads aloud. "Remember to wash your hands, cover your face and make space to reduce infections." This is a helpful reminder.'

'If you would like to go over to the next desk, please,' Ollie tells her. 'It shouldn't be too long before you are seen.'

Sophie thanks him and walks towards Jay, who is standing by the small queue, helping to maintain the two-metre distance rule.

'Please stand behind the white line.' he instructs. After a few minutes, he gestures to the next nurse, and Sophie heads in her direction.

♦♦♦♦♦♦♦♦

Dimple is going for a walk with Kitty, her tiny brown fluffy-eared poodle. Today they are walking up a hilly field. The air is cool, and a fresh breeze is blowing over Dimple's face. She clasps Kitty's lead firmly in her hands and looks up to see what is on the billboard. She usually likes reading it.

'Hands – Face – Space,' It says today.

Dimple heard those exact words on the news yesterday. She also saw the blue arrows on the supermarket floor when she went with Mum. A blue-coloured 2M inside a white circle. Dimple kept the 2

---

[11]Space refers to social distancing.

metres distance throughout. Today, however, only a handful of people pass by as she strolls along with Kitty.

It's good to have the message everywhere as a reminder, Dimple thinks. She starts singing as she trots on with Kitty:

Hands – Face – Space

*Do not forget Kitty*

Hands – Face – Space

*Our PM says*

Hands – Face – Space

# CHAPTER 18

## HANDS – FACE – SPACE ... AND FRESH AIR - 'CAN I GO TO THE MALL PLEASE?'

*April 2021*

Prime Minister Boris Johnson is on the news again.

*"Good afternoon and welcome to this press conference on what has been a big day for many of us, with the first chance to see friends and family outdoors, whether as six people or two households... I must stress that it is only because of months of sacrifice and effort that we can take this small step to freedom today... yesterday we recorded the lowest number of new infections for six months... Now that we have vaccinated more than 30 million adults across the United Kingdom... the evidence seems pretty clear that vaccinating the elderly and vulnerable has helped to drive down rates of hospitalisation and death.*

> *"We want to reinforce that protection with a second dose, so, for many people, April will be the 'Second Dose Month' ...and then, of course, there is one other way we can all build our own individual defences against Covid and enjoy ourselves at the same time – and that is to take more exercise... I am personally thrilled that I will be able to play tennis...*
>
> *"...outdoors is generally much safer than indoors, and the way to continue on our cautious but irreversible roadmap to freedom is to follow the rules and remember, hands, face, space and fresh air[12].'*

Mum heaves a huge sigh of relief. 'Finally! A light at the end of a very dark tunnel.'

'I believe these times will pass,' Nana adds, before turning to drink the rest of her tea.

♦♦♦♦♦♦♦♦

Adam is back on the football field in his first match, a friendly game with the neighbouring team – the Black Rovers – since the lockdown. He and his friends are happy to be playing together again.

---

[12] Published 29 March 2021, [Coronavirus (Covid-19) GOV.UK]

*Hands – Face – Space ... and Fresh Air -
'Can I go to the mall please?'*

'Hey! Ollie!' Adam shouts as he passes the ball to his friend, tackling along the freshly cut grass on the fields. Ollie passes the ball to Adam as they do some warmup kicks.

The referee blows his whistle, and the game commences. Dad is watching from the side-lines, alongside lots of other families. It is a lovely sunny day.

'Go on, Son!' Dad shouts, whistling through his fingers.

The game ends in a 1-1 draw.

Meanwhile, Mum has an appointment to visit the hairdressers with Nana Patricia. 'Ready, Nana?'

'Ready as I can be!' Nana replies happily. 'I have waited so long to see this day.'

Mum drives to Jade's small salon.

Jade and her stylist are wearing masks and visors. 'Mrs Robinson 1 and Mrs Robinson 2! It's wonderful to see you again,' She says with a friendly, welcoming smile.

'I am the original Mrs Robinson,' Nana announces.

'I am the young and pretty Mrs Robinson,' Mum rebuts.

'It's been ages, Jade,' Nana carries on.

Jade collects their light jackets and hangs them on the coat rack. 'Almost fifteen months. Please take your seats.'

Mum sits in the chair at Jade's station and Nana takes her seat with the other stylist.

'How have you coped under lockdown?' Mum asks her.

'Your salon was locked every time Gloria and I drove past this area,' Nana adds. 'We often wondered how you were doing.'

'It has not been easy,' Jade replies. 'Luckily, I applied for the furlough scheme, which has kept my business alive. Thank God for the government initiative to help small business owners. I don't know how I would have survived, otherwise.'

'Was the furlough easy to get?' Mum asks, looking straight at Jade in the mirror.

'There were lots of forms to fill but I was successful with my application. Unfortunately, I had to lay off the new girl who joined me in December 2019. I only have one stylist now. By the way, how did you both manage your hair in lockdown?'

'Wigs,' Mum says. I previously found them uncomfortable but since lockdown gave me no choice, I got used to wearing them for long periods.'

Jade chortles. 'You and most of my clients.' She runs her hands through Mum's hair, trying to unpick the hair at the root.

'I cut mine short,' Nana replies, settling back in her chair with her eyes closed. 'I must say I quite enjoy washing my hair every day.'

'Even 'Bojo' finally got a haircut the other day,' Mum points out.

Nana opens her eyes and looks across at Mum. 'Who is Kojo?'

Mum laughs. 'Bojo, Nana, not Kojo. That's the Prime Minister's nickname.'

Nana laughs until tears run down her face. 'Are you people saying our PM has roots in Ghana?'

'I would have charged him triple for that cut after such a long time,' Jade says, laughing.

'Yes, his hair went wild, didn't it?' Mum chuckles, too. '"Like Spaghetti," one of the journalists said. You are not wrong about the price of that initial haircut either, Jade. The first time James went to his barber, the man charged him double because his hair had grown into a huge afro.'

Jade winks at her in the mirror. 'I'll take a hint from that, then!'

'Don't you dare.' Mum says light heartedly.

Jade changes the topic. 'Boris made history during this pandemic with something else.'

'How is that?' Mum asks.

'He is the first Prime Minister to have a baby while in office.'

'Tony Blair had a son during his office term, too,' Nana points out.

'But Tony Blair was married.' Jade says, applying shampoo to Mum's hair.

'You mean, that woman is not his wife?' Nana blurts out. 'What sort of example is that to young people like Dimple?'

'Nana!!!' Mum retorts.

But Nana will not be shushed. 'It's the plain truth.

Adele, the other stylist, giggles and tries to change the subject. 'By the time we finish styling your hair, you will both look stunning and set off on an adventure like Thelma and Louise!'

'Be careful what you say, Adele.' Mum warns. 'Nana has a naughty streak!'

They all laugh and settle down.

'How is your family?' Mum asks Jade.

'Thankfully, they are all fine. This week, I started practising the new Hands, Face, Space, Fresh Air[13]" slogan with my little daughter. I have been taking her to the park to meet her grandparents and some of the other parents from her school.'

♦♦♦♦♦♦♦

At home, Dimple is getting ready to go to the mall with her friends.

---

[13] The "Hands, Face, Space, Fresh Air" message warns of the dangers of gathering indoors. Ventilation is essential when it comes to reducing the spread of the virus.

*Hands – Face – Space ... and Fresh Air -*
*'Can I go to the mall please?'*

She dons a blue t-shirt and blue pair of jeans and slips on her white and blue Vans trainers. Nana did a rough job of her plaits which are held together at the back of her head with a blue scrunchie. She runs across the corridor to Dad's study. He is working from home today.

'Dad, can I have money to buy some summer t-shirts and new hair clips, please?'

Dad looks up from his monitor and smiles. 'I suppose. Will you be okay going out with your friends on your own?'

Dimple rolls her eyes. 'Of course, Dad. I'm in big school now, and the mall is only one bus ride away.'

Dad reaches for his wallet and hands over a twenty-pound note. 'Have your phone switched on throughout.'

'Sure, Dad. Thanks!' She shuts the door and dashes off to meet her friends at the bus stop.

'Dimple!' Zainab exclaims. 'It's been ages.'

Dimple bumps elbows with her friend and they smile. 'Nearly two months.'

'Is that all? It seems like much longer because we're in different schools. It's such a change from seeing each other every day in primary school.'

'Who is keeping us waiting today?' Dimple asks, putting her arm through Zainab's. 'Not me, for once.'

'Natalie and Amara will join us soon,' Zainab replies, and they sit down to await their friends and the bus.

Natalie hurries towards them, out of breath. 'Hi girls,' She pants. 'Sorry I'm late. It's the twins again! They were crying, insisting that I bring them along.'

'Why didn't you?' Dimple asks with a straight face.

Natalie shakes her head vigorously. 'You must be joking. Do you really want two screaming girls following us around the mall?'

'Not that your Mum would allow you to take them out, anyway.' Zainab pats the seat next to her. 'Sit. And where is Amara, for goodness' sake?'

Dimple grabs her phone from her little bag. 'I'll call her.' But it goes to voicemail.

*Hi! You've reached Amara, please leave your message after the beep and I'll call you later.*

'Now, what do we do?' Zainab grumbles. 'We need to leave immediately so we can do our shopping and get home before it gets dark.'

The other two nod. 'I have to be back to babysit the twins.' Natalie reports. 'I only have a couple of hours.'

Dimple leaves her friend a voice mail. 'Hi Amara. We're leaving now as the bus is here.'

The girls get on the 64 bus and show the driver their 11-15 Zip Oyster photocards which gives them free travel. The bus is not busy, and everyone is wearing a mask. The seat directly behind the driver has been sealed off so no one can occupy it, and alternate passenger seats have been cordoned off to comply with the social distancing rules.

*Hands – Face – Space … and Fresh Air -*
*'Can I go to the mall please?'*

The girls head upstairs, choosing to sit on either side of the front row to get a good view of the town. The high street is a shadow of its old self, and several shops have closed down.

'How are you two enjoying your new school?' Dimple asks.

'We like some of the teachers,' Zainab says. 'Natalie is in the higher group for Mathematics, but we are in the same class for the other subjects.'

'You are both lucky. Mum takes me to school every morning, but I come back on the school bus. I do have a new friend in the same form.'

'What's her name?' Natalie asks.

'Sophia. She is half-Romanian and half-Chinese.'

'You'll still be our friend, though?' Zainab asks Dimple, looking at her with puppy eyes.

'Of course! We're BFFs[14]!'

Natalie turns from staring out of the window. 'Do you get lots of homework?'

Dimple sighs loudly. 'Loads and loads! 'Mum won't let me watch TV until I have finished. If she is at work, Nana supervises to make sure I've completed all my assignments.'

Dimple presses the buzzer, and they get off at the first stop. The mall is on the same side of the road, and they enter through the side door beside the bus stop.

---

[14] Best Friends Forever.

Dimple rushes forward, then turns around to look at the girls. 'Can we go to KFC first? I'm starving!'

'Sure, I'm hungry too,' Natalie says. 'I haven't eaten a thing since lunchtime yesterday. Things were too hectic at home.'

'Hmm, the mall seems to have undergone some refurbishment,' Zainab says, examining the map by the entrance. 'KFC is on the first floor. Let's go!'

The girls travel up the escalator, looking around at the shops. So many shops are still closed, some permanently, judging by the whitewashed windows and boarded doors.

Dimple sighs. 'It's so nice to be together again.'

Natalie lets out a small grunt of agreement. 'I never thought I would say this, but I have missed Mrs Jones.'

'Me too. I guess she prepared us for secondary school life by giving us all those assignments.' Zainab replies, scrolling through her phone.

'Even though we hated her at the time!' Dimple chips in.

*'I expect to have your assignment submitted online by 8am on Monday morning*!' Natalie mimics Mrs Jones so accurately that the other girls burst out laughing. Arm in arm, they stroll towards KFC.

'Two pieces of chicken and French fries, please.' Dimple says to the girl behind the counter who is dressed in the red polo shirt uniform, with a black baseball cap which covers her hair. A hairnet is visible above her ponytail.

'We'll have the same, please.' Natalie and Zainab sound like an echo as they speak at the same time. Dimple has really missed their outings so much. She turns and gives each of them a hug. Natalie would normally shy away from such public displays of affection, but lockdown and the pandemic have mellowed her somewhat.

'Don't get all mushy with me,' she tells Dimple. But there is no heat in her words. She probably feels the same but cannot articulate it.

Dimple glances up behind the counter. There is a menu list with the prices on a screen. She is just calculating how much her meal will cost when the girl at the counter says the most shocking words she has ever heard.

'I'm sorry, but we have run out of chicken.'

The restaurant doesn't have many customers in there since they are still adhering to social distancing rules. Even so, a deafening silence falls across the shop at her words. Then there are a few titters of laughter from the customers.

Dimple looks at Natalie. Then at Zainab. Both girls are standing with their mouths wide open. 'Did I hear you right?' Natalie finally says. At the same time, her friends are speaking.

'What?? No chicken?' This is Zainab.

'No chicken? At KFC?!' Dimple's voice rises as she utters the words. She can't contain her shock. No chicken at KFC is like McDonald's having no hamburgers, or

Pizza Hut running out of dough! She stands there for a few moments, unsure what to say next.

After she thinks it through, she sighs. 'What can we have with our fries, then?'

'We have a selection of meat-free alternatives,' The girl offers.

'I never thought I would see the day when KFC runs out of chicken!' Natalie says.

Dimple orders three portions of fries and meat-free alternatives. Zainab and Natalie take out their purses and hand over some money to Dimple, who then pays for everyone.

Zainab wrinkles her nose. 'I wonder what that will taste like?'

Natalie goes off to reserve a table and sits down while Dimple and Zainab bring the food over. Natalie bites into her sandwich first. The others await her verdict. She is the pickiest eater of the three and her opinion always counts the most.

She chews briefly, pops a fry into her mouth and then bites into the meat-free sandwich again. 'You know what,' she says between mouthfuls, 'I don't notice any difference in taste with this meat-free alternative!'

Zainab looks dubious, but she takes a small bite. Her eyes light up and she turns to Dimple. 'Wow, it's actually delicious!' Dimple needs no more convincing.

'Here goes nothing!' She takes a deep breath, cuts off a piece, places it in her mouth and begins to chew. 'Mmm. It isn't bad.'

*Hands – Face – Space ... and Fresh Air -*
*'Can I go to the mall please?'*

The girls continue eating and filling each other in on what's been happening over the past two months. They finish their meal and walk to the other end of the mall. The mall is a shadow of its old self, many shops are locked. It's hard to believe that this time last year, Dimple and her friends attended the opening of a new bookshop right where they are standing. The bookshop has a sign outside the door: '*This shop is closed until further notice.*'

The girls take the escalator back to the ground floor.

'Oh no!' Dimple exclaims. 'Guys, look at the queue outside Primark!'

'Are we ever going to get in at this rate?' Zainab sounds concerned. Dimple wonders if she is apprehensive because of the crowd. The infection rate is still high, as not every age group has been vaccinated. Those who have been vaccinated are anxious because they are protecting others who refuse to take the vaccine.

'The sooner we queue up, the sooner we can get into the shop.' Natalie says pragmatically. She looks like she is mentally rolling up her sleeves, preparing to do what it takes to get in. She steps into line. Dimple falls in behind her and Natalie stands beside Dimple. They perch their face masks under their jaws and each girl starts playing with her phone.

After a few minutes, Dimple pipes up. 'Why are we the youngest in this queue?'

Zainab looks puzzled. 'What do you mean?'

Natalie chuckles. 'Dimple, you are so funny. People of all ages come to Primark!'

Soon it is time to go in. The girls place their face masks on correctly.

'How old are you?' The security guard asks when they reach the front of the queue.

'Twelve,' Dimple announces proudly.

'You're too young to get the vaccine,' He says.

'We are not here for the vaccine,' Dimple replies. 'We are here to do some shopping.'

'This queue is for the under 30s to get their vaccine,' He explains. 'The queue for Primark is by the side entrance.'

Natalie groans. 'You mean we were in the wrong queue all the time?'

They trot off to the side entrance, at the back of the queue again. After what seems like forever, it is finally their turn. The girls enter the store through the sliding doors. Two uniformed security guards stand by the entrance. The sea-blue Primark logo, inscribed with 'look good, pay less', is visible at the top of the shop.

'Let's go on the escalators,' Natalie says excitedly.

Dimple has a different plan. 'I want to start on the ground floor where the ladies' items are.' The others agree and they start wandering around.

Moments later, Dimple picks up a T-shirt. 'What do you think of this pink T-shirt with the 'LOVE' inscription on the front?'

*Hands – Face – Space ... and Fresh Air -*
*'Can I go to the mall please?'*

'It's dope!' says Zainab.

'OMG! I want that t-shirt too!' Natalie exclaims.

'Do you think I can try it on?' Dimple asks.

Natalie points to the back of the store. 'The fitting rooms are shut.'

Zainab is rummaging through the jewellery racks. She picks out a thin, pretty silver necklace with blue stones. 'Look at this! It's only £2.99.'

Dimple balances the T-shirt on her shoulder and starts searching through the headbands section. She plucks out a pink one. 'What of this headband? It matches the T-shirt.'

'I like the floral headband.' Natalie says, examining one with daffodils layered on a pink background. 'That's two pink things you've picked out there, Dimple. Isn't lilac your favourite colour?'

Dimple smiles. 'I am simply trying out a new look.'

'I prefer the black one.' Zainab says.

'We need a shopping basket.' Dimple announces, laughing. 'We were so excited to finally be in a store that we forgot we would need to put our shopping somewhere! I'll get one from the entrance.' She runs off and soon returns with a basket.

Zainab hands over the items she's picked so far. 'Here you go.'

Dimple collects Natalie's shopping as well and the basket starts to fill up.

'We can go on the escalators now,' Natalie says, thirty minutes later.

They arrive at the first floor. The refund counter is at the back and the customer tills are to the right, opposite the escalator. Dimple is horrified by the long queues of customers waiting to pay for their shopping. But it doesn't matter. She will enjoy the experience, long queues or not.

'This floor is full of men's stuff,' Zainab comments beside her.

'Let's just look around,' Natalie says. 'We have nothing better to do.'

They meander towards the home furnishings.

Dimple lifts up a lilac cushion with a poodle on its cover. 'I love this! And it's available in lilac! I'll ask Mum to get one for me.'

Natalie tilts her head to one side and gives Dimple a look. 'Yup. I didn't think your pink phase would last.'

'I knew it! Lilac is in your system,' Zainab says at the same time. The three girls fall into fits of giggles.

They stroll around the shop, admiring tops, sandals and other lovely items. Two trips up and down the escalator later, Dimple picks out two beautiful hair clips, and they head over to the customer service tills.

# CHAPTER 19

## FAMILY HOLIDAY –
## 'ARE WE BACK TO NORMAL?'

***August 2021***

The Robinsons are going on a Staycation to Oban, a small town located in Argyll and Bute, Scotland. Nana studied in Scotland and still has friends there. They visit as often as possible, but it has been a while, for obvious reasons.

Dad is checking the oil in the Campervan. Adam is loading their suitcases into the back of the vehicle.

'It's going to be a long drive,' Dad says, completing the final engine checks. He closes the bonnet and comes round to assist Adam.

'I'm just glad travel is finally allowed between England and Scotland,' Adam replies, stacking his suitcase on top of Dad's. It's a bit of a squeeze storing everyone's luggage in the boot.

Just then, Dimple makes an appearance, skipping and running excitedly to the van. She is wearing the pink 'LOVE' T-shirt she bought from the mall and a pair of grey leggings. Mum has taken out her plaits. Today, her natural hair is tied up in a neat bun with a pink headband. There is a grey clip on either side of her head.

She is carrying Kitty in her arms, with Kitty's travel bag draped around her shoulder. The puppy has yellow ribbons around each ear, and she keeps trying to lick Dimple's face.

Dimple stashes the bag in the boot and hops into the van, chattering all the while to Dad. 'I can't wait till we get to Oban. I also can't believe this is the second summer holiday during the pandemic. This is *definitely* more exciting than last summer, though.'

Dad nods. 'It's a momentous milestone on the way out of Lockdown.'

Nana walks over and takes her seat in the back of the Campervan. 'Let's pray for good weather!' she says hopefully. 'We have lots of people and places to see.'

'I'm looking forward to visiting the Oban War and Peace Museum.' Adam says.

Mum hands Dad the last of the suitcases. 'And I shall be visiting the castles with Nana. Dimple, I hope you packed your sweatshirts and jumpers.'

'You'll need all of them, Poppet.' Dad adds.

'But I have the new T-shirts I bought from the mall.'

Nana leans forward in her seat. 'You know what the weather is like in Scotland, love. You should take your Dad's advice and get some jumpers, young lady.'

'Alright then.' Dimple hurries back inside the house. Mum follows her to check that all the doors and windows are locked.

'We are getting ready to leave the house now,' Mum is telling Aunty Nadia on the phone when they come back out. Aunty Nadia will be joining Dimple and the rest of the family in Scotland with her three boys.

'We'll see you in two days.' Aunty Nadia replies.

Soon, everyone is seated comfortably in the Campervan, and Dad makes a start on the 400-mile drive to Scotland via the A1 motorway. The journey will take between seven to eight hours, but there will be stops along the way for comfort breaks.

Adam is in the front seat next to Dad; Dimple sits in the middle seat beside Mum and Nana occupies the back row. Dad drives along the city road, surrounded by tall buildings and all sorts of people who seem to be in a hurry.

'Are things back to normal now?' Dimple asks.

'I guess the answer to that will be, "what is normal"?' Adam replies.

'You can't answer a question with another question, Adam!' Dimple retorts, and they bicker happily for a few minutes.

Mum and Dad exchange glances in the mirror and she gives him a signal. Dad gives her a wink and nods. Their children arguing enroute to a family holiday after such chaotic and unpredictable times is a blessing.

'Alright, you two, pack it in!' He finally interjects. 'We're not even ten minutes into the journey! Dimple, it's probably easier to ask what has made the most impact on each of us in the past eighteen months or so. That might be simpler to answer.'

Everyone falls into a thoughtful silence.

They soon leave the city behind, and Dad drives along the country lanes. They travel to Yorkshire, then divert through the Dales towards the North. They pass through River Ure, and the atmosphere is serene and peaceful. Dimple oohs and aahs at the beautiful greenery, with sheep scattered here and there.

Then Dad joins the motorway, and suddenly, piles of cars and vans build up on either side of their Campervan.

'The pandemic has promoted tourism within the UK.' Dad says. 'More families are getting to know more about beautiful places in our country.'

'I can't even bear all the hassle at the airports anymore,' Nana adds. 'Give me a nice trip in a Campervan any day.'

'Especially with self-isolation and quarantine rules still in force.' Mum agrees.

Nana leans forward to tap Dimple on the shoulder. 'To answer your question, it will take a long time for travel to return to normal. All these new tests and travel forms might put many people off travelling. As for what it's meant to me: I have learned not to add unnecessary stress to my life, to be grateful for every blessing and not take people for granted. The verse, "Let everything you say be good and helpful so that your words will be an encouragement to those who hear them,[15]" sums it up for me.

'Yes! I loved shopping for Aunt Mable, Nana.' Dimple exclaims. 'She smiled every time we dropped off her shopping at her doorstep. We saw more of her during lockdown than in all the years we've been neighbours.'

'Exactly!' Nana continues. 'Being good to our neighbours, friends and family members is what counts. If we do that, we obey the commandment "Love thy neighbour as thyself[16]". Listening to the Queen's speech and the quality time we spent as a family during the VE weekend to remember the 'Victory in Europe Day' was also wonderful.'

'I learned several things during lockdown, too.' Adam chips in. 'I will no longer put off doing something that can be done immediately. Final grades were based on assessments instead of examinations. If I had been more consistent with my coursework, my grades would have been better. At least, I can put my volunteering at the vaccination centre on my CV, which is cool. My

---

[15] Ephesians 4:29 (NLT)
[16] Mathew 22:39 (KJV)

grades will get me into military training, for which I am grateful.

'Yes, Son. I am proud of you and your grades.' Dad interjects, patting Adam on the shoulder.

'For me, this experience has confirmed that I made the right decision to train as a nurse,' Mum says. 'I originally wanted to be a flight attendant because air hostesses wore bright uniforms. But now, I wear a uniform and exercise my calling to help people at their lowest point. It gives me great joy when a patient gets better and returns to their families, although many did lose their loved ones, and babies never got to go home to their parents.'

Another contemplative silence falls over the campervan. Dad turns on the radio, and they enjoy some music as he drives along. Soon enough, Dimple's head rolls onto Mum's shoulder. She is fast asleep.

'The virus tested our courage, knowledge, faith and resilience.' Mum says in a low voice. 'Young, active people and old folks gave up the fight against the deadly disease.'

Dad nods, glancing at Mum in the rear-view mirror. 'The virus exposed hidden issues like the disparity in death rates between black and white people. I am also glad that key workers are no longer taken for granted,' He adds.

'Dimple, did you bring Kitty's food bowl along?' Nana asks.

Mum turns around and whispers. 'She is asleep.'

Dad changes lanes, preparing to exit the motorway for the services. 'Can you believe how Nadia's boys have grown? The last time I saw them; they were all so small. Now Samuel especially has shot up like no one can imagine.'

'I can't wait till they join us in Oban,' Adam adds.

Just then, Dimple wakes up and looks around. 'Are we there yet?'

'Not quite,' Dad says. 'You need to be patient, but we'll arrive soon enough.'

'What were you saying, Adam?' Dimple asks.

'We were all reflecting on the effects of the pandemic.' Adam replies, returning to the earlier topic.

'Oh! I learned a lot, too.' Dimple says, rubbing her eyes. 'For one thing, I want to be a nurse like Mum and help sick people get better. I am also happy that I had a party, saw my school friends and got lovely presents. I particularly loved the gold chain from Dad.'

Dad drives into Barton Park Motorway Service Area where the family stop for a rest break.

Mum gives a relieved sigh. 'I can stretch my legs at last!'

'I need the loo.' Nana says, making her way out of the vehicle.

'We are only stopping for fifteen minutes.' Dad shouts. 'Everybody should be back by 2:15.'

Mum puts her arm through Nana's and begins to walk in step with her. 'I'll come with you, Nana.'

'I'm going to McDonald's!' Dimple announces.

Adam, who is retrieving his iPad from his backpack, perks up when he hears that. 'Get me a Big Mac, please. I don't feel like leaving the campervan.'

'Meal or sandwich?'

'The meal with a large Sprite.'

Dimple walks into McDonald's and places her order at the till. 'One strawberry milkshake, one Big Mac meal with a large Sprite, and one apple pie, please.'

'We've run out of strawberry milkshakes,' The crew member, a young man, informs her.

Dimple is astounded. *First KFC, now McDonald's?* 'Really? 'Alright, may I have a vanilla milkshake instead?'

'We have no milkshakes at all,' he replies, 'They are out of stock.'

'Just the Big Mac meal with a Sprite and an apple pie, then.' Dimple says dazedly.

She pays and steps aside to wait. After a few minutes, her number is called, and she collects her order. On her way out, she picks up some serviettes and walks back to the van.

'Dad, you won't believe what just happened.' She says as she gets in.

'What, sweetie?'

'I ordered a strawberry-flavoured milkshake, but there was none. Then I ordered vanilla, but the guy said they had NO MILKSHAKES AT ALL!'

*Family Holiday – 'Are we back to normal?'*

Nana returns to the van with Mum. 'What are you talking about?'

'Dimple wants a milkshake, but McDonald's has run out.' Dad replies.

'Lord have mercy!' Mum says, laughing. 'No milkshake for my Princess?'

'I guess things are not back to normal, after all.' Dimple says.

## THE END

# Wings of Hope

# GLOSSARY

[1] Ear, Nose and Throat Specialist

[2] (There'll Be Bluebirds Over) The White Cliffs of Dover; Words by Nat Burton and Music by Walter Kent (1941–42)

[3] The Freedom Pass allows anyone over 60 to ride for free on public transport at certain times of the day.

[4] Published 23 March 2020 Source, Gov.UK

[5] An unofficial term describing a cluster of people outside households with whom people were comfortable spending time during the pandemic.

[6] The National Health Service

[8] Intensive Care Unit

[10] Source - Sky news, October 2020

[11] Space refers to social distancing.

[12] Published 29 March 2021, [Coronavirus (Covid-19) GOV.UK]

[13] The "Hands, Face, Space, Fresh Air" message warns of the dangers of gathering indoors. Ventilation is essential when it comes to reducing the spread of the virus.

[14] Best Friends Forever.

# BIBLIOGRAPHY

"What is a Covid-19 'bubble' and how to do it safely." 27 Jun. 2020, https://www.cnbc.com/2020/06/27/what-is-a-covid-19-bubble-and-how-to-do-it-safely.html.

*Personal Protective Equipment (PPE)*. (n.d.). Retrieved 10 29, 2021, from http://www.hse.gov.uk/toolbox/ppe.htm

*Dimple Dares to Ask*

# ABOUT THE AUTHOR

Bola Dada is an Information Professional and Chartered Librarian. She is married, lives in London and has two adult children.

Bola is a family-oriented, avid reader who enjoys travelling and meeting both successful people and good role models.

*Dimple Dares To Ask* is her first novel.

www.ingramcontent.com/pod-product-compliance
Lightning Source LLC
Chambersburg PA
CBHW030302100526
44590CB00012B/483